Ya Gotta BELIEVE!

Also by Michael Lichtenstein

The New York Giants Trivia Book

Ya Gotta BELIEVE!

• The 40th Anniversary New York Mets Fan Book •

MICHAEL LICHTENSTEIN

St. Martin's Griffin
New York

www.stmartins.com

Book design by Michael Collica

All photos courtesy of Lewis Requena

Library of Congress Cataloging-in-Publication Data

Lichtenstein, Michael.
    Ya gotta believe! : the 40th anniversary New York Mets fan book / Michael Lichtenstein.—1st U.S. ed.
      p. cm.
    ISBN 0-312-28686-4
    1. New York Mets (Baseball team)—History. I. Title.

GV875.N45 L53 2002
796.357'64'097471—dc21

                                2001057899

First Edition: April 2002

10 9 8 7 6 5 4 3 2 1

Contents

History of the Mets

JUST ANOTHER SEASON

Many New Yorkers mourned the loss more than they would a death in the family. The unthinkable had happened. In 1957 the New York Giants pulled up stakes from the Polo Grounds and the Dodgers from the sacred soil of Ebbets Field; two years after the beloved bums of Flatbush finally beat the hated Yankees in the 1955 World Series, and three years after the heroes of the Polo Grounds swept the Cleveland Indians in the 1954 World Series.

Brooklyn Dodgers owner Walter O'Malley had been lured by Los Angeles to move the team to the West Coast for the 1958 season. If anything, O'Malley was a keen businessman and the city of Los Angeles promised O'Malley a magnificent new stadium with unlimited parking. O'Malley knew that for scheduling reasons the National League would not OK the move for only one team to go to the West Coast. They would require another team and O'Malley talked Horace Stoneham into moving his legendary Giants to the city by the Bay.

The devious O'Malley decided to play a game of cat and mouse with the city of New York, pretending he wanted to stay in New York and proposing sites for a new stadium for his Dodgers. But, by the end of the 1957 season, the die had been cast; the Giants were on their way to San Francisco and the Dodgers to Los Angeles.

Dodgers and Giants fans were crushed, and felt betrayed. Jay Hoffman, a Washington Heights resident and Giants fan, summed up the feelings of many New York baseball fans when he said, "Summers became different, there were no games to go to at the Polo Grounds. There was something missing, some sweet aspect of life. Summer had just become another season."

In most Brooklyn neighborhoods Walter O'Malley replaced Adolph Hitler as the most hated man in history. Stephen Shestakofsky, who was twelve years old in 1957 recalled that day: "It broke my heart when the Dodgers left. I'm not a vengeful person but I always despised Walter O'Malley for tearing the heart out of Brooklyn."

Some Dodgers and Giants fans swore off baseball for the rest of their lives and others even went so far as to pledge allegiance to the hated Yankees. For most, however, a long dark night that would last four-and-a-half years had begun. The morning would begin, thanks mainly to the efforts of Bill Shea, when the New York Metropolitans took the field for the 1962 season.

A MAN NAMED SHEA

Most acknowledge that the man responsible for the return of the National League to New York was Bill Shea. The Manhattan lawyer was the most active member of the four-man committee set up by the mayor, Robert Wagner, for New York in the fall of 1957. To get another National League baseball team in New York Shea, a Manhattan attorney with some political clout, followed various avenues to accomplish his goal. At first he tried enticing existing National League franchises to move to New York, but, when that failed, Shea lobbied the power brokers of baseball to expand the eight-team setup to ten teams in each league.

The League initially turned down Shea's proposal. But, the bright, energetic Bill Shea took another route. In 1959, he joined forces with Branch Rickey to establish a third professional baseball league that would call itself the Continental League. The franchises would be in Houston, Minneapolis, Toronto, Buffalo, Dallas, Atlanta, Denver, and New York. Though the Continental League never got off the ground, it gave Bill Shea a weapon in attaining his goal.

There was also talk around that time of having baseball's long-standing antitrust laws overturned, which caused trepidation in the baseball world and opened room for thought.

Shea, sensing an opening, announced that if the Leagues would expand by four cities the creation of a Continental League would be stopped. On October 16, 1960, the National League announced that it would expand into two cities, Houston and New York.

Bill Shea won his battle, and a grateful city would pay its due to the man by naming the new stadium after him. Shea Stadium opened in 1964 and has been home to the Mets since.

A LADY CALLED JOAN AND A GUY CALLED WEISS

One of the early investors in the Mets, who eventually garnered eighty percent of the team's stock, was Mrs. Joan Whitney Payson. Mrs. Payson was a fixture in the New York social scene through her various philanthropic causes, as well as her support of the arts and civic charities. She was also a sportswoman who, along with her brother, owned many notable racehorses. But, despite her wealth and blue-blood status, Mrs. Payson never lost her common touch. She rooted for the Mets, sitting behind the team dugout, with the same fervor as the working-class guy in the bleachers.

The "Baseball Guy" behind the fledgling enterprise was George Weiss, who was brought into the fold in March 1961. Despite the designation "club president" Weiss would serve as the new club's General Manager, a role he was abley suited for.

Weiss had served as Yankees GM during the '50s, when the Bronx Bombers captured six World Series championships, but along with his manager he was let go by the Yankees after the 1960 World Series defeat by the Pittsburgh Pirates. George Weiss came on board with the Mets a year before they began their initial season. His manager, a guy by the name of Charles Dillon Stengel, wouldn't be far behind.

THE OLE PROFESSOR IS BACK

He was a legend way before he put on a New York Mets uniform, and took the field as manager of the fledgling team. Charles Dillon Stengel had previously taken the field at the Polo Grounds as a scrappy, competent, outfielder for John McGraw's Giants in the '20s. Stengel later managed the Brooklyn Dodgers in the '30s and won seven World Series as the Yankees manager from 1949–1960.

Casey Stengel, most fans agreed, was an excellent choice to call the shots on the field for the new New York team. Some felt the crusty but earthy Stengel was an icon in the world of New York baseball for he had worn the uniforms of every New York baseball team since the '20s.

If any man was suited to lead the Mets in their initial season, it was the still able seventy-two-year-old Casey Stengel. Writers loved to huddle around Stengel for his insights, witticisms, and quips that made great copy. Once introduced at a press conference as the Mets manager, Stengel took the podium and in his grave voice proclaimed, "I'm glad to be managin' the New York Knickerbockers." The startled audience broke into laughter. They would need a sense of humor and irony to get them through those first years with the Mets.

THE WIT AND WISDOM OF CASEY

Perhaps no manager in the history of baseball has ever been quoted as often as Casey Stengel. Reporters never had to worry about handing in dull copy if they were covering Casey's team. Stengelisms, these from the 1962 maiden season of the New York Mets, are quotes never to be forgotten.

"I don't mind my ballplayers drinking, as long as they don't drink in the same bar as me."

"We have a great young outfield prospect. He's twenty-two and with a little luck he might make it to twenty-three."

"I was the best manager I ever saw."

"I was fired more times than a cap pistol." (Of his managerial career.)

"I want to thank all these generous owners for giving us those great players they did not want."

"If I was winning I'd play five games a day because you tend to keep winning when you are winning. But I had a chance to call this game, so I did. You tend to keep losing when you're losing, you know." (On convincing the umpires to call a game due to weather that the Mets were to play against Houston.)

"Everybody here keeps saying how good I'm looking. Well maybe I do, but they should see me inside. I look terrible."

(Commenting on his appearance after the end of the 1962 season.)

"I find I got a defensive catcher only who can't catch the ball the pitcher throws," on catcher Chris Cannizzarro who Stengel often called "Canzoneri."

"You look up and down the bench and you have to say to yourself, 'Can't anybody here play this game?' "

When Shea Stadium opened in April 1964, Casey took the baton from bandleader Guy Lombardo and led the Royal Canadians in tune before the Mets lost the Shea opener 4–3 to the Pirates. A year later Casey Stengel fell and broke his hip at a party at Toots Shor's famed Manhattan restaurant. The old professor later announced his retirement and was replaced by Wes Westrum, who managed the team in Stengel's absence and had previously served the club as a coach. Charles Dillon Stengel was inducted into the Baseball Hall of fame in 1966. He passed away on September 29, 1975, at the age of eighty-five. Sadly, Joan Payson, the principal owner of the Mets since their inception, also passed away that same week.

THE METS FIELD A TEAM

By the fall of 1961 the Mets were ready to roll. They had owners, a GM, a stadium to play in (the old Polo Grounds and a new stadium under construction in Flushing), and had coaxed the irascible Casey Stengel out of retirement to manage. What they needed now were players. The heads of baseball reassured the fledgling Mets that they would remedy the situation. The National League established a pool of players from the eight existing clubs for the upstart Houston Colt 45's and the Mets to choose from. National League teams could protect all but seven players from their active roster and all but eight players from their minor league farm system. Rogers Hornsby was hired by the Mets to prepare a scouting report on the prospects that were eligible. Hornsby summed up his feelings on the dire prospects when he said, "They say we are going to get players out of a grab-bag, but from what I see it's going to be a garbage bag."

The first player selected by the Mets was catcher Hobie Landrith, who the Mets picked off the roster from the San Francisco Giants. Casey Stengel, being the astute baseball strategist that he was, explained the choice by saying, "Without a catcher you will have a lot of passed balls."

The draft was held on October 10, 1961, in Cincinnati. By the end of the day the Mets had a team—or at least twenty some-odd warm bodies who would play that coming spring at the Polo Grounds. National League baseball was restored to New York after a four-year absence.

THAT FIRST DECADE

The starting lineup for the New York Mets when they stepped onto the field to play the St. Louis Cardinals on April 11, 1962, read as follows:

Richie Ashburn–CF
Felix Mantilla–SS
Charley Neal–2B
Frank Thomas–LF
Gus Bell–RF
Gil Hodges–1B
Don Zimmer–3B
Hobie Landrith–C
Roger Craig–P

Richie Ashburn concluded his distinguished major league career with the Mets in 1962. Though his best years were way behind him, most of them spent with the Philadelphia Phillies in the '50s, Ashburn nonetheless hit a solid .300 that year for the Mets. He would leave the playing field at the end of 1962 for the broadcast booth with the Philadelphia Phillies, where he remained until his death in 1997. Ashburn was inducted into the Baseball Hall of Fame in 1995.

Felix Mantilla was picked up from the Milwaukee Braves where he had been a light-hitting utitlity infielder. He hit .275 and had 11 home runs in 1962.

Charley Neal was a favorite among Mets fans, especially those from Flatbush. Neal had been a young infielder with the Dodgers in their last years in Brooklyn, he was an adequate glove man, he was capable of winning a game with his bat. He hit .260 with 11 home runs for the Mets in 1962. The following season he was traded to the Cincinnati Reds.

Frank Thomas was a journeyman NL slugger when he joined the Mets from the Milwaukee Braves. He hit 34 home runs in 1962, a record that would last for 20 years until Dave Kingman hit 37 home runs in 1982.

Gus Bell had been an integral part of the power-hitting Cincinnati Reds teams of the '50s, but at the age of 33, like Richie Ashburn and Gil Hodges, Bell had his best years behind him. Bell would only manage to hit .149 with 1 home run, but, he had the first hit in Mets history—a single—during that inaugural game in St. Louis. He would finish the season in Milwaukee and end his career with the Braves in 1964.

Gil Hodges, the beloved adopted son of Brooklyn, returned home in 1962. Though the Dodgers had abandoned Brooklyn in 1957 for Los Angeles, Hodges never gave up his Kings County residence. Hodges had been a dangerous power hitter with the Dodgers in both Brooklyn and Los Angeles and a flawless fielder at first base, but injury plagued the 38-year-old Hodges. He would only hit .252 with 9 home runs in the 1962 season. He would be lured away by the Washington Senators to serve as their manager, but Gil Hodges would return.

Don Zimmer was another former Brooklyn Dodger who put on a Mets uniform in the spring of 1962. He played 14 games for the "Amazins" and hit an anemic .077 before going off to Cincinnati. In the spring of 1962, Zimmer set a dubious record when he went 0 for 34 at bat.

Hobie Landrith, though never an all-star, was nonetheless a competent big-league catcher with the Orioles and the Giants. Early on in 1962, Landrith was sent packing for a hard-hitting first baseman by the name of Marvin Eugene Throneberry.

Roger Craig broke in with the Brooklyn Dodgers in their World Series championship year of 1955 along with Al Jackson and Jay Hook. They were the aces of the Mets' pitching staff. Craig turned in a workmanlike season on the mound with 10 wins and 24 losses.

At one point during 1962, when Craig was pitching well but still losing, a teammate commented, "His luck has been so bad that if he bought a cemetery no one would die." Craig's baseball luck would improve in 1964 when he was traded to the St. Louis Cardinals, who won the World Series that year. He would finish his playing career with the Phillies in 1966. In the late '70s he would begin a successful career managing the San Diego Padres and end with the San Francisco Giants in 1992.

A MET AMONG METS

At twenty-eight when most ballplayers are in their prime, Marv Throneberry was traded to the Mets for catcher Hobie Landrith and a love affair began for Mets fans as Throneberry won their hearts.

Throneberry broke in with Casey Stengel's New York Yankees in the 1958 season, but by 1960 he was with the Kansas City A's, and the following year he went to the Orioles. He never seemed to last in one place too long. "Things just sort of keep happening to me," Marv Throneberry once remarked.

Once in a game against the Cubs a miscue by Throneberry let the Cubs score four runs in half of an inning. When Throneberry came to the plate for his next at bat, he was determined to make amends. With two men on base, Marv got a hold of a pitch and took it deep to right-center. Throneberry tore down the first-base line, sprinted past second, and on to third. The Polo Grounds' crowd roared but the cheers seized when an umpire called him out for not touching first. Casey Stengel stormed out of the Mets dugout and began arguing with the ump who had made the heinous call. The second-base umpire ended the argument when he said, "Casey, I hate to tell you this but he also missed second."

Throneberry was slow and often dropped throws to first. He also threw to the wrong base and had a certain knack for rescuing defeat from the jaws of victory. The fans nicknamed him "Marvelous Marv," despite the 120 games lost that season due to countless miscues from Throneberry. Through it all he never lost his good nature or sense of humor. Once when a teammate dropped a pop fly Throneberry playfully chided the player saying, "Hey, what are you trying to do, steal my fans?"

At the end of the season Throneberry was presented with the Good Guy Award by the New York baseball writers. At the presentation Throneberry joked that he was told not to stand too long holding the plaque because he might drop it.

Marv Throneberry hit .244 and 16 home runs for the Mets in 1962. He would never play in the big leagues again, and in 1963 he was sent to Buffalo, but the legend of "Marvelous Marv" would live on. In the late '70s a beer company decided to put together a commercial with a group of rowdy former superstar athletes. Among the notables were Mickey Mantle, Billy Martin, and Bubba Smith of NFL fame, along with other former pro ballplayers.

Toward the end of the commercial the camera panned over to Throneberry who said in a bemused manner, "I still don't know why they asked me to do this commercial." Marv was one of the icons of that horrible but loveable 1962 Mets team. He tried his best, but the Gods of the Diamond always seemed to turn their backs on him. If any man was born to be a Met, it was Marvin Eugene Throneberry (even his initials spelled MET). Marv Throneberry died in his native Tennessee in 1994. He was sixty years old.

THE BOYS IN THE BOOTH

Not only did the Mets have to put a team out in the field, they had to put together a team to broadcast the games. WOR Channel Nine, that had previously carried the Brooklyn Dodgers games, won the rights to televise the Mets. The broadcasting crew, who would later establish a record for longevity in the booth, included Lindsey Nelson, Bob Murphy, and Ralph Kiner.

Nelson, an old broadcasting hand, had previously worked college and pro football game broadcasts but he called NBC's Major League Baseball games from 1957–1961. Nelson was known as a straight-shooter and was often kidded about his colorful sports jackets. "He had a great enthusiasm for the job," Ralph Kiner commented about his colleague. In 1979 Lindsey Nelson left New York to take a job calling San Francisco Giants games. Nelson stayed in San Francisco for three seasons then semiretired. He taught broadcasting seminars at his alma mater, the University of Tennessee, and did some college football broadcasts for the Turner Broadcasting Station. Nelson died on June 12, 1995, in Atlanta, Georgia. He was seventy-six years old.

Bob Murphy joined the Mets broadcasting staff after stints in Baltimore and Boston. His warm, gracious manner entertained and informed Mets fans through the decades. In 1982 Frank

Cashen, the Mets GM, decided to switch Murphy solely to radio broadcasts. It has been said of the native Oklahoman, who once studied Petroleum Engineering at the University of Tulsa, his pace is upbeat and slamming players is not his style. Murphy was inducted into the Broadcaster's Wing of the Baseball Hall of Fame in 1994. He joined Nelson and Kiner, who was inducted as a player.

Most New York baseball fans knew of Ralph Kiner way before he ever sat behind a microphone. In the late 1940s and early '50s Kiner was a prodigious slugger for the Pittsburgh Pirates. During the years between 1947 and 1951 Kiner averaged nearly 47 home runs and 121 runs batted in a year, a score rivaled only by the immortal Babe Ruth. Kiner averaged 7.1 runs per 100 at bats while the Bambino averaged 8.5. Such feats landed Kiner in the Hall of Fame, but most Mets fans also see the craggy faced Kiner as a Hall of Fame broadcaster as well.

Mets president Fred Wilpon once reflected, "No one knows more about baseball than Ralph does."

Kiner has enthralled Mets fans throughout the years with his baseball yarns, and he has made countless games and players of past eras come alive in his good-natured anecdotal tales. Though sometimes the names and places run array, consider these "Kinerisms" part of the total wonderful package that Ralph brought to the Mets broadcast booth.

Though both Kiner and Murphy are in their seventies now, Mets fans hope that they'll continue to broadcast Mets games for many years to come.

WHAT COULD HAVE BEEN

Players came and went in those early years and while the Mets picked up a number of ballplayers who had All-Star seasons, and Hall of Fame careers, most were brought to the Mets long after their All-Star prime.

From 1962–1968 the following players' names were found on the rosters of the New York Mets.

Richie Ashburn: Ashburn concluded his fifteen-year career with the Mets hitting a team-leading .306. The fleet centerfielder had a .308 lifetime batting average and was inducted into the Baseball Hall of Fame in 1995.

Gil Hodges: Hodges left his best playing days behind him at Ebbets Field. The slugging first baseman once belted four home runs against the Boston Braves in a 1950 game. He ended his career hitting 370 dingers and with a respectable .273 batting average in a career that spanned from 1947 to 1963. Hodges hit .252 for the Mets with 9 home runs in the 1962 season. Most New York baseball fans felt Hodges's omission from the Hall of Fame is a major injustice.

Clem Labine: Another Kings County darling, this former Flatbush fireman was the ace of the bullpen for the pennant-winning Dodgers teams of the 1950s. He posted 77 wins, 96 saves, and a respectable ERA of 3.63 during his thirteen-year career. Labine called it quits after the '62 season and returned to his native Rhode Island. Labine appeared in only 3 games for the Mets, but posted a hefty ERA of 11.25 that season.

Duke Snider: A legend in his time, the "Duke of Flatbush" came back to New York for the 1963 season, but the sweet swing had left the Duke. Though he left the game with a .295 career batting average and 407 homers, Snider only managed 14 home runs and a .243 batting average for the Mets in 1963.

Jimmy Piersall: This colorful, slick-fielding ball hawk was a mainstay at Fenway Park for the Boston Red Sox in the '50s. Piersall went six for six in a 1955 game and led the American

League in doubles with 40 in 1956. Piersall is best remembered, however, during his brief career with the Mets for running the bases backward when he hit his 100th home run off Dallas Green. The Mets released Piersall soon after that home run. He was hitting a dismal .194. He would rebound the following year with the Los Angeles Angels, where he hit .314.

Frank Lary: He was known as a "Yankee Killer" because of his success against the Bronx Bombers. Lary twice posted twenty-game winning seasons during a career that spanned a dozen years. His top mark was 23–9 in 1961. The Alabamian ended his career with the Chicago White Sox in 1965, scoring 128 wins with a 3.49 lifetime ERA. His 1964–1965 stats with the Mets were 3–6 in 27 games.

Yogi Berra: This Yankee icon, as most know, also served the Mets as a coach, and later as manager but, how many remember Yogi as a player for the Mets in 1965, or more appropriately player-coach? The Yankees fired Berra after his first one-year stint managing the Bronx Bombers in 1964. The firing was surprising because although they had lost to the St. Louis Cardinals in the World Series the team had still won the AL pennant that year. The Mets wasted no time in signing the beloved New York baseball figure. He would bat nine times that season and get two hits before becoming a full-time coach.

Warren Spahn: This left-hander won 363 games during a career that began with the Boston Braves in 1942. His manager then, as it was in 1965, was Casey Stengel. Spahn once remarked, "I'm the only guy to play for Stengel both before and after he became a genius."

Warren Spahn was forty-four years old when he took the mound at Shea Stadium for the Mets in 1965. He would win four games and lose twelve for the Mets before finishing his career with the San Francisco Giants later that year. Spahn, the winningest left-hander in the history of baseball, would be voted into the Hall of Fame in 1973.

Ken Boyer: The Mets acquired the Cardinals' Ken Boyer, one of the greatest third basemen in the history of the National League, for pitcher Al Jackson at the end of the 1964 season.

Boyer would join his younger brother, Clete, who held down third base for the Yankees. Boyer was voted the National League's MVP in 1964 when the Cardinals captured the World Series from the Yankees. Both Boyer brothers swatted home runs in game seven, the first time that feat was ever accomplished. Ken Boyer whacked 287 career home runs and batted .287 during his 14-year career. Ken Boyer hit .266 and 14 home runs for the Mets in 1966. He would go on to play with the White Sox and the Dodgers. Ken Boyer would retire in 1969 and later manage the St. Louis Cardinals.

Dick Stuart: This fun-loving slugger made a brief appearance with the Mets in 1966. Stuart was a vital cog on the Pittsburgh Pirates team of the early '60s, including the World Championship winners of 1960. In 1961 Stuart bashed 35 home runs, knocked in 101 runs, and hit .301. Stuart bettered his home run mark with the Red Sox in the pitcher's year of 1963 when he belted 42 home runs and hammered in 118 runs. Both marks led the American League in 1963. In his 1966 season with the Mets, Stuart hit .218 with 4 home runs. He would later play with the Dodgers and California Angels. Later, during a season in Japan he quipped, "Nothing bothers me anymore after being the only American player on a team in Hiroshima."

THE MET WHO WAS TRADED FOR HIMSELF

Harry Chiti was a journeyman catcher in the 1950s and '60s. He finished his career with a .238 batting average. Chiti had stints during his eleven-year career with the Cubs, the A's, the Tigers, the Senators, the Twins, and the Mets. The Mets got Chiti from Detroit in 1962. The price the Tigers asked was a "player to be named later." Harry Chiti appeared in 29 games that year and hit a meager .195. At the conclusion of the 1962 season Harry Chiti was sent packing back to Detroit as the "player to be named later."

SOWING THE SEEDS

The year 1968 would be cataclysmic for America. The war in Vietnam raged with no end in sight, students rebelled on campuses over the war, and hippies talked about "peace and love." America was horrified by the murders of Robert Kennedy and Dr. Martin Luther King, and Richard Nixon was elected the thirty-fifth president of the United States.

That year was also the one when things began to change for the New York Mets. The beloved son of Flatbush, Gil Hodges, returned home from his exile in Washington where he managed the lowly Senators to respectability and New York fans hoped he would would perform the same miracle for the Mets. Hodges made it known early on that losing was unacceptable. First Baseman Ed Kranepool reminisced, "He changed the attitude from clownishness to playing baseball."

The Mets fielded one of the youngest teams in the National League. Under Hodges they finished the 1968 season with a best team record ever, a 73–89 mark, and a ninth-place finish.

The 1968 Mets finished the season with a paltry .228 team batting average. The mainstay of the team were the young arms, which included Jerry Koosman, with a team record 19 wins, Tom Seaver, with 16 wins and 205 strikeouts, and a young Texan by the name of Nolan Ryan who, though slowed by injuries and military service, managed to strike out 133 batters in 134 innings.

On the field the Mets had Tommy Agee, a power-hitting centerfielder who they acquired in December 1967 from the White Sox where he had been the American League Rookie of the Year for the 1966 season. The youth movement was soon to pay dividends. The best seasons were ahead for outfielder Cleon Jones, shortstop Buddy Harrelson, second baseman Ken Boswell, catcher Jerry Grote, first baseman Ed Kranepool, and outfielder Ron Swoboda. The major players were in place for that most magical of season of Mets baseball yet.

1969 MIRACLE IN QUEENS

Though the Vegas odds-makers had the Mets at 100–1 to take the 1969 World Series, a new feeling came over Mets fans and players that year. Though the nucleus for the 1969 squad had been put in place during the 1968 season, there were still moves the Mets had to fine-tune for their 1969 product.

The Mets obtained Wayne Garrett that winter from Atlanta. The twenty-one year old was looked upon as having solved the troublesome problem at third base. The Mets also picked up Donn Clendenon from Montreal. Hodges would platoon the right-handed slugger with lefty hitter Kranepool throughout the 1969 season.

The team got off to a lackluster start. After a quarter of the season had gone by, the Mets record was still below five hundred and they were nine games behind the league-leading Chicago Cubs. Then lightning struck. From May 28 to June 10 the Mets went on a tear, winning eleven straight games and boosting themselves from fifth place to second, hot on the trail of Leo Durocher and his Cubs. The Mets took four out of six from the Cubs in July and the Shea faithful felt something special was happening in this most interesting of baseball seasons, 1969.

1969: DOWN THE STRETCH

The Mets floundered in July, playing below .500 and some Mets fans of questionable faith thought the Mets had made their run prematurely in June.

By mid-August the Mets were mired in third place, 9½ games behind the Cubs, but then lightning struck again. The Mets magic kicked in and they won 38 of their remaining 49 games. Pitching was the team's strong suit and Shea Stadium crowds cheered the mound mastery of Tom Seaver, Jerry Koosman, rookie Gary Gentry, and the sound relief pitching of Tug McGraw. Koosman, at twenty-six, was the old man of the group.

Once again, the Mets bested the Cubs in an early September series at Shea. A few days later, on September 10, the Mets took first place from the Cubs by beating Montreal. David had beaten Goliath once again. Mets fans wondered if this newfound magic would last or would the Mets, America's favorite sad sack of losers, tumble from grace.

COULD THIS BE FOR REAL?

As the war in Vietnam still raged, and John Lindsay campaigned for his second term as mayor of New York, the Mets hung on to their first-place lead and finally clinched it on September 24, 1969, beating, the Cardinals 6–0 behind the shutout pitching of Gary Gentry.

At season's end the Mets were the hottest team in baseball, having won 38 of their last 49 games and hitting the 100-win mark. The Gods of Baseball smiled benevolently on the Mets. Fans could point to the September 15th game against the the St. Louis Cardinals as proof of a blessed team. Steve Carlton, the Cards pitcher, had his fastball going and though he struck out 19 Mets, the Mets nonetheless prevailed 4–3 on two two-run home runs by Ron Swoboda. Mets fans celebrated the night of September 24 as they captured their first National League East pennant. But, Mets fans knew there were two more obstacles in their path before the impossible dream was realized. The first obstacle would be the Atlanta Braves, whom the Mets would face in their first National League Championship Series appearance. If the Mets were victorious against the Braves, they would battle the winner of the American League Championship Series, which that year was the Baltimore Orioles.

MOVING ON TO THAT IMPOSSIBLE DREAM

The Mets opened the best of five series against the Braves in Atlanta. The Braves were lead by the fabled Hank Aaron, who that year had smashed 44 home runs and batted .300, and Rico Carty who batted a sizzling .342.

The Mets pitching staff would have to be on top of their game to cool off the hot Atlanta bats.

The Mets went with their ace Tom Seaver to start the opening game of the National League Championship Series. He faced Phil Niekro, who posted 23 wins for the Braves during the 1969 season.

Though Seaver was not at his best the Mets battled and scratched out a hard-fought 9–5 win. The next day Jerry Koosman took the mound and the Mets bats came alive as the

"Amazins" scored in each of the first five innings, taking a 9–1 lead. The Braves showed signs of life scoring five runs in the fifth inning and chasing Koosman off the mound, but relievers Ron Taylor and Tug McGraw dispatched the Braves, and the Mets once again prevailed 11–6.

With the Mets sporting a 2–0 lead in the series, the action shifted back to Shea. Mets fans hoped to end the series at home and their wishes were granted as the Mets, with the pitching of twenty-two-year-old Nolan Ryan and a home run by rookie Wayne Garrett, bested the Braves 7–4. New York celebrated the sweep of the Braves, but all knew that a bigger celebration would follow if the Mets were to beat the Baltimore Orioles. For the first time since the Brooklyn Dodgers and New York Yankees locked up in the classic 1956 series, a New York National League baseball team would take part in the World Series. New York fans awaited the start of the Series.

TALE OF THE TAPE

The smart money in Vegas had the Orioles pegged to capture the World Series in 1969. After all the Orioles were a team that boasted 109 wins during the regular season. They had two pitchers, Mike Cuellar and Dave McNally, that both had 20 wins that season, and Jim Palmer who chalked up 16 wins and a gaudy 2.34 ERA. After a distinguished career Palmer would win election to the Hall of Fame in 1990.

The Orioles starting eight was star-studded. Lead by the Robinsons, Frank clouted 32 home runs, banged in 100 RBIs, and hit an impressive .308 while Brooks patrolled the outfield. Both Robinsons, like Jim Palmer, would enter the Hall of Fame. Frank would be the first African-American to manage in the big leagues, taking over the reins of the Cleveland Indians in 1975.

The Oriole lineup included the massive Boog Powell, who thumped 37 round trippers during the 1969 season; Paul Blair, played center field and hit .285 with 28 home runs; Mark Belanger, a defensive gem at shortstop; and a steady solid second baseman by the name of Davey Johnson, who Mets fans would get to know better in the years to come.

The Mets faced the Orioles with a pitching staff that included Tom Seaver, who took the NL's Cy Young Award as he posted a 25–7 record with 208 K's and an ERA of 2.21. The ace southpaw of the staff was Jerry Koosman, who won 17 games; and the youngster was Gary Gentry, who chalked up 13 wins. Nolan Ryan, whose season had been shortened by military commitments and injuries, intrigued Met fans with a 6–3 mark and struck out 92 batters in only 89 innings. The bullpen was manned by Tug McGraw and Ron Taylor, giving the Mets a stalwart lefty–right combo.

Cleon Jones lead Met hitters with a .340 average and Tommy Agee led Mets batsmen with 26 home runs. The Mets team batting average was a lackluster .242, compared with the Orioles average of .265.

The Orioles banged out 175 home runs, compared to the Mets who had only managed 106, and Oriole baserunners swiped 82 bases compared to the Mets 66.

Overall, the Orioles had more hitting, speed, and power than the Mets, but the Mets had fate on their side.

THE AMAZIN' DREAM REALIZED

The 1969 World Series opened on a bright sunny Indian Summer day in Baltimore. With Tom Seaver and Mike Cuellar facing one another, the Orioles took an early lead when Don Buford parked a pitch by Seaver over the right-field wall. The Orioles coasted to a 4–1 win over the Mets. Orioles fans smiled a "told you so" at the upstarts from the Big Apple and some Mets fans began to wonder if the dream was over, but there was a quiet confidence amongst the team. The confidence emanated from their manager Gil Hodges. The Mets didn't sulk after that loss; instead their confidence level rose. Seaver said he felt buoyed rather than shaken and said the feeling on the club was that they could take the Orioles. The Mets anxiously awaited Game Two.

Jerry Koosman got the nod to start the second game. Koosman, the Minnesota farm boy, who legendary New York sportswriter Dick Young once referred to as a "Cool Cat" because unlike most pitchers he was at ease and would often joke with sportswriters and teammates on the dugout bench on days he was pitching. Koosman was supremely confident that there wasn't a hitter he couldn't get out. But, the Baltimore Orioles had other ideas, sending Dave McNally to the mound in a battle of southpaws.

Donn Clendenon gave the Mets the lead with a solo home run in the fourth inning. Koosman's pitching was flawless and he had a no-hitter going for him in the seventh inning, with a 1–0 lead. The Orioles tied the game and ruined Koosman's no-hitter, but the Mets were not to be outdone. Base hits by Ed Charles, Jerry Grote, and Al Weis gave the Mets a 2–1 lead when Ron Taylor came in at the bottom of the ninth for the save and a Mets win.

Game Three moved to Shea Stadium and a crowd of 56,335 welcomed the Amazins home. In the crowd were such New York luminaries as Jackie Kennedy Onassis and her son John F. Kennedy Jr., Governor Nelson Rockefeller, Mayor John Lindsay, and even Yankee icon Joe DiMaggio. Steve Lawrence sang the national anthem and the beloved Roy Campanella, of Brooklyn Dodger fame, threw the opening pitch.

The Mets took an early lead in the first inning as Tommy Agee started the Mets off with a home run in the first inning. The Amazins continued with a 5–0 lead in the seventh inning.

The Orioles loaded the bases off of a pitch by Gary Gentry. Nolan Ryan came into the game in relief of Gentry to face Paul Blair. Blair sliced a fastball into the alley between center and right. Tommy Agee made an incredible diving, sliding grab that kept the Orioles from getting back into the game. Earlier Agee had made a spectacular one-handed grab at the base of the left-field wall to rob catcher Elrod Hendricks of an extra base hit with two on in the second inning.

The Mets shut out the O's 5–0 with Gentry picking up the win and Ryan earning the save, but it was the defensive play of Agee that saved the day.

Oriole manager Earl Weaver commented after the game, "I've never seen two such catches by the same player in the same game." There would be more heroics in the 1969 World Series as the Mets took a 2–1 lead.

COULD *THIS* BE FOR REAL?

The fourth game of the 1969 World Series was another pitcher's duel between Tom Seaver and Mike Cuellar. The game stood 1–1 in the tenth inning and once again the Baseball Gods smiled on the Mets.

Jerry Grote led off the bottom of the tenth with a fly ball that Paul Blair lost in the sun. Grote ended up on second base, but was taken out by manager Gil Hodges for little-used outfielder Rod Gaspar. Bud Harrelson was walked intentionally, giving the Mets runners on first and second. Pete Richert bore down to pitch to second-string catcher J. C. Martin, who bunted the ball back to Richert, whose throw hit Martin going down the line. The ball ricocheted to right field, and Gaspar, running with the pitch, scored the winning run from second.

As in Game Three, a Mets outfielder saved the game. This time it was Ron Swoboda in right field who dashed Orioles' hopes for a big ninth inning when he speared a sinking line-drive, holding the Orioles to a lone run.

A record crowd of 57,397 came out to Shea Stadium to witness the fifth, and most hoping, final game of the 1969 World Series as the Mets flirted with baseball immortality.

Jerry Koosman, who won Game Two of the Series, opened for the Mets on the gray, overcast fall day. The Mets trailed 3–0 in the bottom of the seventh as Koosman and Dave McNally battled one another. The Orioles' lead was cut to 3–2 by solo home runs from Clendenon and Weis. Ironically, it was the light-hitting Weis's first home run at Shea Stadium in two years. Behind the hitting of Ron Swoboda and Cleon Jones, who both doubled, and the Orioles' miscues, the Mets took a 5–3 lead into the eighth inning.

The Mets were three outs away from the impossible dream. In a year that had seen a man walk on the moon, a bitter New York mayoral race between John Lindsay and Mario Procacino, and a city split by the war in Vietnam, at 3:17 P.M. on October 16, 1969, Davey Johnson, the Baltimore second baseman, flied out to Cleon Jones in left field and the New York Mets were World Champs. And New York if not the world was a little bit happier that day.

AFTERMATH

The crowds rampaged onto the field at Shea in the euphoria of the Mets' championship. Cleon Jones battled through crowds of well-wishers and revelers to the clubhouse where he jubilantly acknowledged, "Some people still might not believe in us, but then some people still think the earth is flat."

New York prepared for its biggest celebration in years. The Mets were the darlings of the nation. They were David who had just triumphed over Goliath. They were all New Yorkers and the city went wild.

New York threw their heroes a ticker tape parade down Broadway and over a million fans took part in the gala. Later that day, Mets manager Gil Hodges took part in a salute to the Mets in downtown Brooklyn at Borough Hall. Hodges thrilled the crowd by putting on an old Dodgers jacket, reminding many that the last time a New York National League team had won the World Series was fourteen years earlier, when the Dodgers beat the Yankees.

CONTENDING

As the new decade began, New York had definitely become a Mets town. With stars like Seaver, Koosman, Agee, Jones, Grote, and McGraw returning, New York baseball fans had visions of more pennants and World Series in their baseball dreams. And although the Mets were in contention during the 1970 season, fueled by the hitting of Clendenon and Agee, they finished third, six games behind Pittsburgh Pirates.

The Mets batting was even livelier than it had been in 1969 with an average of .249, besting the 1969 average of .242, but the Mets fell down on what was the team's centerpiece, its pitching. There were some brilliant efforts during the season, such as Tom Seaver's masterpiece against San Diego on April 22, 1970, when he fanned 19 Padres and ended the game by striking out 10 Padres in a row. Seaver ended the season with 18 wins, but other members of the Mets pitching staff, who had helped carry the team to the championship the year before, weren't as fortunate. Koosman was limited to 12 victories by arm woes. Gary Gentry was also off with only 9 wins. Nolan Ryan, though possessing a fastball that enthralled Mets fans and would eventually put him in the Hall of Fame, was nonetheless mired in a 7–11 season.

Changes had to be made. The Mets got rid of third baseman Joe Foy, who had hit a weak .243, and picked up Bob Asporomonte from the Braves. Also gone was 1969 Series hero Ron Swoboda, who was dealt to the Montreal Expos for centerfielder Don Hahn. A rookie by the name of Ken Singleton, a powerful switch-hitting outfielder and Queens native made it up to Shea through the Mets farm system. He hit .245 and had 13 home runs in his rookie season.

Despite the moves, the growing emergence of Seaver as one of the games' top pitchers, and legitimate superstars, the Mets could not repeat the magic of 1969.

The Mets had now been in existence ten years and their fans had suffered through the horrendous early years, soared to the peak of ecstasy during their championship season, and now faced the reality of pulling for a team somewhere in the middle of the National League pecking order. That wasn't good enough for the Shea faithful. Mets fans, always strong on optimism, looked to the acquisition of American League All-Star shortstop Jim Fregosi, whom the Mets would move to third base for the 1972 season.

The Mets acquired Fregosi from the California Angels by trading them Nolan Ryan, who Mets brass felt would never reach his potential or cure his wildness.

Their was optimism in the Mets camp as the 1972 season was beginning, and then tragedy struck.

On April 2, 1972, Gil Hodges and his coaches were returning to their motel in West Palm Beach, Florida, after completing a round of golf when Hodges collapsed and died of a fatal heart attack. Hodges was only forty-seven years old. New York and the baseball world mourned for the strong, silent Hoosier who loved New York, especially Brooklyn, and was loved back by the city he adopted.

HERE COMES YOGI

There was a pall on the 1972 Mets with the sudden death of Hodges, but the season would go on. The team needed a manager to lead them and another beloved New York legend was tapped for the job, Yogi Berra.

Berra had worn Yankee pinstripes as a player and a manager from 1946 to 1963. He had been a perennial All-Star catcher on Yankee teams that won 14 pennants and 10 World Championships during his playing career. At the end of the 1963 it was decided by the Yankees that Berra would manage the Bronx Bombers for the 1964 season.

Though the Yankees won the pennant with Berra as coach, he was sacked by the Yankees when they lost the World Series.

Though a shrewd and astute student of the game, his image in many quarters of the New York sports world was that of a comic due to his butchering of a phrase or two which newspapermen were fond of reporting. These malapropos became known as "Yogisms."

"That place is so busy no one goes there anymore."
"Take it with a grin of salt."
"It ain't over 'til it's over."

With Lawrence Peter Berra at the helm for the Mets, management also decided to make changes on the field. They sent Ken Singleton, Tim Foli, and little-used first baseman Mike Jorgensen packing to Montreal in exchange for Rusty Staub, one of the top hitters in the National League. Not long after, another outfielder joined the Mets, and though he had departed New York at the end of the 1957 season, he was a large part of New York baseball tradition and one of the greatest players who ever played the game.

WELCOME BACK WILLIE

On May 11, 1972, the Mets acquired fabled Willie Mays from the San Francisco Giants for pitcher Charlie Williams and cash. It had been twenty-one years to the day that Mays had arrived as a rookie at the Polo Grounds, launching his fabled career. Though the forty-one-year-old legend's skills had diminished since his days with the New York Giants, Mays still had a sentimental pull for fans. He reflected the Golden Era of New York baseball and had been the centerpiece of the long-raging feud between New York baseball fans who debated the merits of centerfielders Duke Snider, Mickey Mantle, and Willie Mays.

Mays welcomed his return to New York by calling it "A Return to Paradise." Many fans felt with the return of the "Say Hey Kid" came a return to the days when New York was the mecca of Major League Baseball.

The Mets soared in the early part of the 1972 season, playing better than .700 ball in early June. Mays slugged a home run to win a game against the Phillies in his first start with the Mets to continue the pace to the pennant, but injuries to Cleon Jones, Jerry Gote, Bud Harrelson, and Rusty Staub caused the Mets to drop to third place at season's end.

Though the Mets finished in third place in 1972 there were some bright spots during the season. Pitcher Jon Matlack who finished with 15 wins and a 2.32 ERA was voted National League Rookie of the Year. Tom Seaver posted 21 wins and outfielder Rusty Staub hit a respectable .293 before a broken hand put him out of the lineup for the major part of the season.

On the short side, most Mets bats went anemic during the season, with a team batting average of .225. Mays hit .267, but it paled to his previous accomplishments: the "Say Hey Kid" was a shadow of his former self.

The Mets began preparing for 1973 in the off-season by send-

restore order. As the action between the combatants died down, Cincinnati relief pitcher Pedro Borbon emerged from the fray wearing Mets pitcher Buzz Capra's cap. When Borbon realized it, he tore the hat off of his head, bit it, and then ripped it apart.

When the game continued, Mets fans pelted Rose, who was playing left field, with anything they could get their hands on. Cincinnati manager Sparky Anderson ordered his team off the field until civility could be restored. The Mets were threatened with forfeiture, but calm was restored, or a semblance thereof, and the game continued. With that win the Mets took a 2–1 lead in the series.

The Reds and Rose achieved some payback in Game Four. Despite fine pitching by Stone and McGraw the Reds won 2–1 with Pete Rose hitting the winning home run in the twelfth inning. During the game Mets outfielder Staub separated his shoulder crashing into the outfield wall as he made a spectacular catch.

The crucial fifth, and deciding, game saw Tom Seaver take the mound against Jack Billingham. Though Seaver was not his usual sharp self, the Mets nonetheless took a 7–2 victory and the National League flag.

The Mets would play the Oakland A's in the 1973 World Series. Once again they would be the underdogs but it was a role the Mets seemed to thrive on. The Mets made their second World Series appearance in five years. For manager Yogi Berra, it was a highlight as he joined Joe McCarthy as the second man in Major League Baseball history to manage pennant winners in both leagues.

The A's were a team filled with rebels and All-Stars. The star studded lineup included AL MVP rightfielder Reggie Jackson, shortstop Bert Campaneris, leftfielder Joe Rudi, third baseman Sal Bando, and catcher Gene Tenace.

The A's also had the arms to go along with the heavy "Catfish" Hunter had 21 wins as did Kenny Holtzman, Vida Blue chalked up 20 victories, and ace reliever Rollie Fingers posted an impressive 1.91 ERA during the '73 season.

The series began in Oakland on October 13. Jon Matlack and Kenny Holtzman pitched against one another in a 2–1 Oakland win.

The Mets as they had so often done during the 1973 season, bounced back in Game Two with a sloppily played 4-hour-and-13-minute-game, though the Mets finally bested the A's in 12 innings. The win was tinged with bittersweet, as Mets fans saw the forty-two-year-old Mays fail to come up with a fly ball that fell in for a double and allowed Oakland to tie the game 6–6 in the bottom of the ninth. Mays-watchers knew that Willie would have easily put the ball away with one of his famed basket catches only a couple of years earlier. Time had finally caught up with the "Say Hey Kid." Willie Mays would never take the field again in a big league game. In the twelfth inning of that game, Mays bid farewell to baseball as he singled in the go-ahead run with two outs. The Mets scored three more runs and bested the A's 10–7.

Game Three moved back to Shea. The Mets took a quick 2–0 lead in the bottom of the first but lost 3–2 in extra innings. Seaver started for the Mets, Catfish Hunter for the A's. Harry Parker gave up the winning run in the top of the eleventh and was pinned with the loss. Paul Lindblad picked up the win for A's with the incomparable Rollie Fingers picking up the save.

The Mets roared back in Game Four as Rusty Staub bashed a three-run homer in the bottom of the first. He would end up with five RBIs in the game as Matlack pitched eight innings of three-hit ball. Matlack and Staub were key in the Mets to 6–1 win.

The boys from Shea had a 3–2 Series lead after Game Five as ᴐsman and McGraw combined for a three-hit shutout. Cleon ᴉs and Don Hahn provided timely hits in the 2–0 triumph. The now stood on the threshold of claiming their second World ᴉionship.

A's evened up the series in Game Six as Catfish Hunter ᴐɴᴇd Tom Seaver, 3–1.

The deciding game of the 1973 World Series would be a dual between two southpaws, Jon Matlack and Kenny Holtzman.

The light-hitting Campaneris took a Jon Matlack pitch downtown and gave the A's a 2–0 lead. The lead soon doubled as "Mr. October," Reggie Jackson, lived up to his name, slamming another Matlack pitch over the fence to make the score 4–0. Harry Parker came on in relief for Matlack, but the damage was already done. The Mets never rebounded from the 4–0 deficit. Oakland won the game 5–2 and took the 1973 Championship.

Though the Mets came up short it was nonetheless a season Mets fans would look back in later years with pride. A gutsy, battling Mets team lacking power, hitting an anemic .246 with no 20-game winner on their pitching staff had copped the NL flag and came within a game of taking it all. Mets fans could hardly wait for 1974.

LOST IN THE PACK

The Mets finished fifth in the NL East in 1974, 17 games behind the Pirates who took the flag. Once again the Mets put a light-hitting team on the field. Not one Mets starter hit .300 or had more than 20 home runs. The team bottomed out with a pathetic .235 batting average. If those facts weren't sad enough, the vaunted Mets pitching staff also started to fall apart. Seaver, bothered by a hip injury, finished with an 11–11 record. Jon Matlack had a losing season at 13–15, but led the Mets with a team high seven shutouts, and a low ERA of 2.41. Jerry Koosman was the high man with fifteen wins, which was a terrific accomplishment considering the lack of run support, and a relief staff whose top man was Harry Parker with a paltry four saves. Tug McGraw suffered through a horrible season. The mirthful left-hander only posted 3 saves and a bloated 4.15 ERA. McGraw got tagged with eleven losses.

During the off-season of 1974–1975 the Mets acquired Joe Torre. The Brooklyn native returned home at 34, but Torre's skills had diminished from his days with the Braves and the Cards. It was with the Cards in 1971 that Torre hit a league-leading .363 with 24 round-trippers. John Stearns, a young catcher from the Phillies, came to Shea as the Mets traded fan favorite Tug McGraw. Perhaps the biggest pickup for New York came from the West Coast Giants.

The guy's name was Kingman and few that met him would ever forget him. To say Dave Kingman was moody, and maybe a bit strange, would be an understatement. He didn't talk to too many people and he lived on a boat with a dog, but he could hit home runs of massive proportions. In 1975 Kingman struck out 153 times and only hit .231 but blasted a then-team record 36 home runs. He supplied the power in a very resurgent Mets lineup as the bats woke up and pitching returned to Shea.

Along with Kingman's team-leading 36 home runs, Rusty Staub tallied 105 RBIs, Ed Kranepool hit a career high .323, and rookie Mike Vail came up to the big club and hit .302.

On the mound Tom Seaver returned to form with a 22–9 record and Matlack and Koosman also rebounded by winning 30 games between them. Reliver Bob Apodaca chilled NL hitters with a 1.48 ERA and 13 saves.

But, despite the renaissance, the Mets finished in the middle of the NL East pack in third place, 10½ games behind the Pirates.

There had been other changes made during the 1975 season as well. Manager Yogi Berra was replaced by Roy McMillan in August, and Cleon Jones, a hero from the 1969 and 1973 pennants, was shown the gate.

The heroes of the glory years were becoming history as the Mets struggled in the mid-'70s. During the off-season Mets fans mourned the passing of Mrs. Payson, the lady who, along with Bill Shea, was one of the prime movers in bringing the NL back to

New York. The owner of the Mets from their inception, Payson passed away on October 4.

The 1976 Mets sported a few new looks. Joe Frazier called the shots from the dugout, after managing the Met Triple-A team at Tidewater the year before.

Mickey Lolich joined the team from the Tigers, in exchange for fan favorite Rusty Staub. Lolich would win 217 games during his 17-year career, unfortunately, few of them came during his tenure with the Mets. The stocky left-hander finished with an 8–13 record, and once again the Mets finished in third place. Koosman and Matlack combined for 38 wins with Koosman finishing the year with 21 wins and 10 losses. A contract holdout affected Tom Seaver during 1976. He finished with only a 14–11 record, but still cooled NL hitters with a 2.59 ERA. The Mets lineup didn't terrorize too many pitchers in the NL. There were no .300 hitters in the lineup and no power besides Kingman, who managed to belt 37 round-trippers despite missing a quarter of the season. Shadows were descending on Shea Stadium. Across town in the Bronx, the Yankees began to flex their muscles and would soon dominate the American League for the remainder of the decade. During those years the Mets would descend to the depths of the National League.

THE SAD YEARS

The relationship between Seaver and Mets chairman M. Donald Grant also continued to cool. Grant never forgave Seaver for holding out at the beginning of 1976 and the relationship continued to fester. On June 15, 1977, the unthinkable happened. "The Franchise," as Seaver was often called, was traded to the Cincinnatti Reds for infielder Doug Flynn, outfielder Steve Henderson, first baseman Dan Norman, and pitcher Pat Zachry. Though Henderson proved to be an able hitter after putting on a Mets uniform and Doug Flynn would wow Mets crowds with his glove work in the infield, it would be years before Mets fans came to terms with the loss of Seaver.

On that infamous day of June 15, the Mets also unloaded power hitter Dave Kingman to the San Diego Padres for pitcher Paul Siebert and infielder Bobby Valentine.

The Mets finished last in the NL. Joe Frazier was KO'd with little more than a quarter of the season gone and was replaced by Joe Torre.

Torre retired as a potent player, with a .297 batting average. He assumed his managerial duties in mid-June and though Torre would show his mettle as a championship manager two decades later with the Yankees, the Mets did no better for Torre than they did for Frazier. There were a few heroes on the 1977 Mets. Scratch hitter Len Randle batted .304, catcher John Stearns and first baseman John Milner tied Henderson for the home run lead with 12. Nino Espinosa, a twenty-four-year-old right-hander from the Domican Republic, led the once powerful Mets pitching staff with a mere 10 wins. Mets fans hoped for better things in 1978.

During the off-season, Bud Harrelson was sold to the Phillies and Felix Millan, who many Mets watchers thought of as the greatest second baseman in team history, left for a stint in Japan.

There was little to cheer at Shea during the 1978 season. John Stearns and Brooklyn's Lee Mazzilli proved to be young talents with their best seasons ahead of them but other than that, there was little for Mets fans to get excited about.

The Mets hit bottom in early May and never rose out of last place during the 1979 season. Attendance reached an all-time low at not quite 800,000. New York baseball fans were staying away from Shea, many opting for the Bronx where the Yankees were trying for a third-straight championship, having beaten the Dodgers in the 1977 and 1978 World Series.

Steve Henderson hit a respectable .306 in 1979 and Craig

Swan posted 14 wins, more than doubling the win total of any other Mets pitcher on the roster. Changes for the new decade would be on the agenda for the Mets. Fans and players alike hoped for a rosier future.

But there still remained little for Met fans to cheer about in the early '80s. Trades would be made that brought back Staub and Kingman, but for both sluggers their best days were behind them. Staub would still be an effective pinch hitter and spot player up into the mid '80s and would go down as one of the most popular players in team history. The Mets sent young reliever Jeff Reardon to Montreal for All-Star outfielder Ellis Valentine. Reardon went on to be one of the top relievers in the NL for a decades, while Valentine never cut it in New York. Joe Torre stayed at the helm of the Mets during the 1980 and 1981 seasons.

The Mets finished fifth in the NL East in 1980, twenty-four games behind the Phillies. The team finished fifth again in 1981. In those two years no Mets hitter had more than 22 home runs for the season.

The top winner in 1980 and '81 was Mark Bombeck with ten wins in 1980. Neil Allen, a young reliever, won 14 games against 16 losses, and posted 40 saves in that two-year span. It didn't take a genius to see that steps had to be taken to return the New York National League baseball team back to respectability.

There was a new skipper at the helm for the Mets as the 1982 season began. GM Frank Cashen tapped Baltimore pitching coach George Bamberger to call the shots on the field and February of that year the Mets pulled off a blockbuster trade with the Cincinnati Reds for slugger George Foster. The Mets paid Foster handsomely for his services. The deal called for a $10-million payout over five years. Mets fans wondered if they finally had the slugging superstar they had dreamed about. In 1977 Foster hit 52 home runs and knocked in 149.

As the 1982 season opened Mets fans looked to the thirty-three-year-old Foster to supply the home runs and RBIs the team needed. But, the Mets were not finished in the trade market. Having unloaded catcher Alex Trevino, pitchers Jim Kern and Greg Harris to the Reds for Foster, the Mets turned their trade attentions to the American League. The Mets unloaded popular outfielder Lee Mazzilli to the Texas Rangers for pitching prospects Ron Darling and Walt Terrell. Despite these personnel moves the Mets once again finished in the basement of the NL East. Mets fans had little to feel good about. Dave Kingman walloped 37 home runs, but the moody first baseman batted a woeful .203 for the season. The heralded George Foster hit just 13 home runs for the Mets in 1982, well off his previous pace. It appeared the Mets had once again reverted back to their old habits of picking up declining superstars.

There was one pleasant surprise for Mets fans in 1982 in the form of outfielder Mookie Wilson. Mookie won many fans that year at Shea with his all-out hustling play. Wilson also surprised Mets fans by stealing 58 bases, an unheard of feat for a player on the previously heavy-footed Mets teams. Wilson provided a spark that year and would be a Mets favorite for many years to come.

The following year, 1983, marked the return of Tom Seaver. Now thirty-eight, Seaver had little mound magic left, but Shea faithful still thronged to the stadium to see "Tom Terrific." Seaver finished 1983 with a 9–14 mark, but moves were being made in Mets land to rise from the bottom of the NL East.

First baseman Keith Hernandez came on board from the Cardinals in exchange for pitchers Neil Allen and Rick Ownbey. Keith Hernandez was the best fielding first baseman in the NL. Having won the NL batting title in 1979 with a .344 average and sharing the MVP award that year with Willie Stargell of the Pirates, Hernandez gave the Mets a legitimate superstar and catalyst to build a team around.

In 1983 the Mets also brought up the much-heralded young

slugger, Darryl Strawberry. Strawberry, the first pick of the 1980 free agent draft, signed with the Mets out of Los Angeles's Crenshaw High School and some in the Mets organization were already calling the teenager a "black Ted Williams." During his rookie year Strawberry clouted 26 home runs, knocked in 97 runs, and batted .257, not Ted Williams stats but prolific for a 21-year-old. Mookie Wilson continued to thrive in the Mets outfield and he continued to be a phenomenon on the basepaths, swiping 54 bases while hitting a creditable .276. The Mets were building a team for the future but their detractors still pointed to their woeful pitching staff. In 1983 their top starters were Ed Lynch, who finished 10–10, and 36-year-old Mike Torrez, but help was on the way in the form of another teenage superman from Florida.

TURNING THE CORNER

Davey Johnson was named new manager of the Mets during the 1983 World Series. Johnson replaced the interim Frank Howard, who had taken the Mets helm after George Bamberger had been fired.

Johnson had been the skipper for the Triple-A Mets club in Tidewater, and he promised a winning season for the big club in 1984. There would be a painful setback along the way. Tom Seaver was lost in the off-season as the Mets failed to protect their future Hall of Fame pitcher on the free agent list, feeling few teams would desire the now thirty-nine-year-old pitcher. But, the White Sox plucked the Mets legend, and Seaver would have a productive 15–11 season for Chicago.

Davey Johnson was a veteran of the strong Baltimore teams from the mid-'60s and early '70s. He knew championships were built on strong, young arms. Johnson looked around that spring training and liked the young pitchers he saw.

There was twenty-three-year-old Ron Darling, newly-arrived

Sid Fernandez from the Dodgers; Walt Terrell, a competitive twenty-five-year old, and the graybeard of the starting rotation, twenty-eight-year-old Ed Lynch. But the ace of the staff would be its youngest member, a teenager from Tampa, Florida, named Dwight Eugene Gooden.

Gooden had been pitching for Lynchburg in the Carolina League where he struck out 300 batters in 191 innings. Davey Johnson took note of Gooden's accomplishments and as Johnson's Tidewater team went into the minor league playoffs, Johnson pulled strings and had Gooden put on Tidewater's roster. The young man didn't disappoint, winning two of his three starts and Tidewater won the League Championship.

Gooden headed north to the Mets for the season opener of the 1984. Mets GM Frank Cashen wanted to send Gooden back down to Tidewater for more seasoning and call him up later in the season, but Johnson knew the Florida right-hander was something special. He convinced Cashen that the kid was ready for the bigs; a conviction that would prove right.

The likeable, confident youngster with an infectious smile won his first start of the season against the Houston Astros. He would total 17 wins that year. Many fans in Shea Stadium were beginning to forget about "Tom Terrific" and were becoming "Doctor K" fans.

Gooden also fanned 276 in 218 innings.

The Mets had their most successful season in 10 years winning 90 games and losing 72. The Mets held a 4½ game lead over the Cubs in late July, but lost the lead as the Cubs beat the Mets in 7 of 8 games in a two-week span in the second half of the 1984 season.

Dwight Gooden was named NL Rookie of the Year but there were many Mets heroes that year. Darryl Strawberry powered 26 home runs, with 97 RBIs in his second season. Keith Hernandez, the league's most polished first baseman, led the team with a .311 average. Foster chipped in to the Mets cause with 24 home runs and 87 RBIs.

The other young pitchers showed promise as well with Darling finishing the season with a 12–9 record and reliever Jesse Orosco recording 31 saves in his fireman role.

The 1984 Mets were a respectable and a contending ball club, but Frank Cashen would make a move in the off-season that would make the boys more than just respectable.

That move came on December 10, 1984, when the Mets acquired perennial All-Star catcher Gary Carter from the Montreal Expos. Mets fans rejoiced, but the hard-hitting catcher did not come cheap. Montreal received infielder Hubie Brooks, a productive hitter and a Mets fan favorite along with catcher Mike Fitzgerald, outfielder Herm Winningham, and pitcher Floyd Youmans.

The Mets never possessed a catcher with Carter's abilities. Outside of his 30-plus home run seasons, Carter was excellent at handling pitchers and possessed a bazooka for an arm.

Also joining the Mets roster before opening day 1985 would be the veteran third baseman Ray Knight, who had struggled the year before with the Astros. The Carter trade paid dividends immediately. Gary Carter's tenth-inning home run against the Cardinals in the season opener gave the Mets an opening game win against the team that would be their main rivals for the NL East flag.

The Cards bested the Mets for the 1985 NL East flag with a team built on speed, defense, and pitching. Vince Coleman, the Cardinal outfielder, stole 100 bases and fellow outfielder Willie McGee hit .353 and took the NL MVP award. John Tudor and Joaquin Andujar each won twenty-one games to pad the Cardinals three-game lead over the Mets. When the season ended the Mets posted 98 wins and had their supply of heroes as well.

Doc Gooden was the most dominant pitcher in the major leagues that season. The twenty-year-old Gooden put up 24 wins against 4 losses. At one point in the season Gooden tossed 14 straight wins and ended the season with a sizzling 1.53 ERA, easily taking the NL Cy Young Award. Ron Darling also proved a force to be respected on the mound. The former Yalie put in 16 wins against 6 losses and was named to the NL All-Star team along with Gooden. Keith Hernandez led Met batsman with a .309 average, had 24 game-winning hits, and an eighth-straight Gold Glove.

Behind the plate the Mets reaped the dividends of the Carter deal. Gary Carter swatted 32 home runs and knocked in 100. Darryl Strawberry hit 29 home runs, despite missing seven weeks with torn ligaments in his thumb. Rusty Staub, in his last season, aided the Mets with 11 pinch-hits before hanging up his cleats to go into the restaurant business.

Mets fans showed their appreciation for the team's 1985 season by returning to the stadium in droves—2,751,437 Mets fans went through the turnstiles at Shea setting a then-record for New York baseball attendence. Mets fans saw good baseball in 1985 and they expected even more for the 1986 season.

HAIL TO THE CHAMPIONS

The Mets ran hard throughout the 1986 season and led the pack until they clinched the flag on September 17. When the season ended the Mets had 108 wins with only 54 losses, the third-best win-loss record in the history of the National League.

Manager Davey Johnson set the tone early in the season when he issued a challenge to his team and the National League saying, "I don't want to just win the division, I want to dominate it." The acquisition of lefty pitcher Bobby Ojeda, who came over from the Red Sox and won 18 games, and Kevin Mitchell, who came up from the Mets farm system and provided versatility on and off the field, helped propel the team.

The Mets stumbled coming out of the gate, losing three of their first five but the team soon righted itself and began to run roughshod over the rest of the NL. By the end of April the Mets had a five-game lead over their rivals. The team's confidence and swagger grew to such an extent that adversaries considered the Mets players to be arrogant and cocky, adding an impetus to beat the boys from Shea. But, few succeeded.

Whitey Herzog, the manager of the 1985 NL pennant-winning St. Louis Cardinals, announced the race for the NL flag was all but over and proclaimed the Mets the winners at the end of June as they stormed to a 50–21 record.

The 1986 Mets were a team of many contributors. Third baseman Ray Knight had an inspirational comeback-year hitting .298 with numerous game-winning hits. The gritty Knight provided leadership on and off the field after two sub-par seasons where nagging injuries had laid him low. He took the NL Comeback Player of the Year Award, and those wouldn't be the last of the honors for the Mets third baseman.

Mookie Wilson suffered an eye injury during the season and center fielder Lenny Dykstra filled the vacancy. The aggressive, go-for-broke, tobacco-chewing Dykstra hit .295 and led the team with 31 stolen bases. When Mookie returned back to the Mets lineup he would find himself platooned with the hard-hitting Kevin Mitchell in left field but made the most of his playing time and hit a solid .289 for the season.

The Mets had five players on the 1986 NL All-Star team. Gary Carter, who was an anchor for the Mets, hit 24 home runs and knocked in 105 runs. Strawberry hit 27 home runs and patrolled right field. Hernandez played a solid first base and took another Gold Glove award for his ninth consecutive year and also hit .310.

The Mets also boasted two All-Star pitchers that season. Dwight "Doc" Gooden continued to be the scourge of National League batsman, finishing with a 17–6 record and striking out 200 hitters. Another Mets pitcher also had 200 Ks, Sid Fernandez, and the southpaw finished with a 16–6 record.

But, for Mets fans, there were more than five All-Stars on the team. Among them were Bob Ojeda, who lead the Mets in wins; and Wally Backman, their switch-hitting second baseman who hit a surprising .320 for the year. Backman was a "table setter," setting the table for many Mets' rallies with his knack for getting on base.

With the combination of experience, youth, speed, power, and pitching the Mets rose to manager Davey Johnson's challenge, dominating the NL East with 108 wins and finishing 21½ games ahead of the second-place Phillies. The Mets would face the tough Houston Astros in an unforgettable National League Championship Series.

The Astros were a team built on solid pitching and sound fundamental play. Their big bopper was first baseman Glenn Davis who belted 31 home runs and knocked in 101 runs. Davis was supplemented in the Astros lineup by outfielder Kevin Bass who hit .312 with 20 home runs during the 1986 season and third baseman Denny Walling, who batted a team-leading .312, but the main nemesis for the Mets would be pitcher Mike Scott.

Scott, a former Met, took the Cy Young Award for 1986 and baffled NL hitters with his split-fingered fastball. He lead the league with 306 K's that season, and also had a 2.22 ERA.

Astros manager Hal Lanier could boast a pitching staff that also included 17-game winner Bob Knepper and the legendary Nolan Ryan. The thirty-nine-year-old former Met was already a legend on his way to Cooperstown. Ryan's fastball hummed: he struck out 194 men in 178 innings.

Manger Hal Lanier decided to go with his Cy Young winner in the first game of the National League Championship Series. Game One was played at the Houston Astrodome and it pitted Gooden against Scott. The game turned out to be the pitchers' duel the experts promised. Scott was flawless, fanning 14 Mets without giving up a run. Gooden was also nearly flawless, but a second inning home run by Glenn Davis gave the Astros a 1–0 lead that they held throughout the game for the win. The Mets evened the series the next game as Bob Ojeda bested Nolan Ryan and the Astros 5–1. Keith Hernandez had the key hit with a two-run triple in the fifth inning that fueled the Mets win.

The NLCS moved to Shea for Game Three. The Mets' confidence in coming home soured as the Astros ran off to a 4–0 lead early in the game. In the sixth inning the Mets rolled up their sleeves and went to work.

Darryl Strawberry hit a massive three-run homer that tied the game, but not for long. The Astros took a 5–4 lead in the seventh inning on an unearned run against reliever Rick Aguilera. Behind 5–4 in the bottom of the ninth, the Mets came back with the volatile Lenny Dykstra. With a man on first and one out Dykstra lined a Dave Smith pitch over the right-field fence for a 6–5 Mets win, giving them a 2–1 advantage in the series. Once again the celebration was short-lived; the Mets would have to face Mike Scott in Game Four.

Scott was in his usual dominating form during the game, putting the Mets down 3–1. The biggest blow was given by Houston catcher Alan Ashby in the second inning, when he took a Sid Fernandez pitch downtown landing a two-run homer. The series was tied once again at two wins apiece. The Mets realized that for a shot at the World Series they would need to win Games Five and Six or they would have to face the indomitable Mike Scott again.

Game Five pitted two phenoms against one another, the fireballer Ryan against Gooden. A crowd of 55,000 witnessed a classic pitching duel.

Houston scored in the fifth and the Mets tied the game in the bottom of that inning with Darryl Strawberry hitting his second home run of the series. After nine innings the game stood at 1–1.

Nolan Ryan was taken out after the ninth inning after giving up only two hits while striking out twelve. Doc Gooden lasted an inning longer and, like the Texan, had given up only a lone run.

Reliever Charlie Kerfeld came on for Houston in the tenth and Jesse Orosco relieved Gooden an inning later. The game

remained deadlocked until the twelfth inning where Wally Black-
man singled and then reached second on a Kerfeld throwing
error. Keith Hernandedz was walked intentionally and now Kerfeld
faced Gary Carter, who had been struggling at the plate during
the series. Carter worked Kerfeld to a 3–2 count then lined a shot
up the middle. Backman scooted home and the Mets had a 2–1
win. One more game was needed and the Mets would be going
to the World Series. The series went back to Houston for Game
Six, possibly one of the greatest playoff games in the history of
baseball.

The Mets and their fans knew that the sixth game of the 1986
NLCS was a do-or-die for the Mets. They would either do it in
Game Six or face Mike Scott and his unhittable split-fingered fast-
ball in Game Seven.

Bob Ojeda faced Bob Knepper in that memorable sixth game.
The Astros worked Ojeda early, reaching him for three runs in the
first inning and after eight innings the Astros held a 3–0 lead. Bob
Knepper was pitching the game of his life but Mets fans began to
hope against hope that there would be no seventh game and no
Mike Scott to face. With three outs to go the Mets needed heroics from the team who never said die. Pinch hitter Dykstra led off
from the ninth inning with a triple and came home on a Mookie
Wilson single. Kevin Mitchell grounded out, but Keith Hernandez
doubled, bringing in Wilson and knocking Knepper out of the
game two outs from a Houston victory.

With Hernandez on second base the Astros brought in their
closer Dave Smith, who notched 33 saves during the '86 season.
Smith wouldn't get number 34 this day though. The Astros
reliever had trouble finding the plate walking Gary Carter and Darryl Strawberry. Ray Knight flied out, bringing Hernandez in to tie
the game at 3–3 and forcing it into extra innings.

The game stood tied until the fourteenth inning as Roger
McDowell pitched in flawless relief during those five innings, yielding just one hit. The Mets manufactured a run in the top of the

fourteenth with Wally Backman knocking in a run with a single. As the teams went into the bottom of the fourteenth the Mets held a 4–3 lead and were just three outs away from going into their third World Series. Jesse Orosco, the Mets ace reliever, would close down the Astros but they did not go quietly.

With one out in the fourteenth, outfielder Billy Hatcher tagged an Orosco pitch and the Mets hearts sank when the ball cleared the wall tying the score 4–4, keeping the game alive as it approached a marathon length. Key hits in the sixteenth inning by Strawberry, Knight, and Dykstra, as well as a wild pitch by Houston pitcher Jeff Calhoun, gave the Mets a comfortable 7–4 lead going into the bottom of the inning. Once again the Mets were three outs away from the World Series. The Astros however had other ideas. A tired Orosco walked Davey Lopes who was then brought home by singles from Jim Doran and the troublesome Mickey Hatcher. With one out in the sixteenth the score stood at 7–5. Denny Walling grounded out, but Glenn Davis singled bringing in Jim Doran. The Mets held a one-run lead and needed all but one out to end the series. It boiled down to a fatigued Jesse Orosco. Pitching against outfielder Kevin Bass, who posted a solid .311 batting average during the season, the wily Orosco made Bass chase breaking balls and with a 3–2 count Bass swung and missed at another Orosco breaking ball. After four hours and forty-two minutes the Mets had bested the Houston Astros and had won their third National League pennant. They would face the Boston Red Sox in the 1986 World Series.

THE SECOND MIRACLE AT SHEA; THE 1986 WORLD SERIES

The Mets would be facing the formidable Boston Red Sox in the 1986 World Series. The Red Sox had bested the New York Yankees by five and a half games to clinch the American League

East and had played a League Championship series every bit as stirring as the Mets.

The Red Sox lost three of their first four playoff games against the California Angels, but came back in dramatic fashion. They won the next three games leading many a Red Sox supporter to think this 1986 team would put an end to the "Curse of the Bambino."

The Red Sox boasted a lineup that included All-Star third baseman Wade Boggs, who hit .357 during that season; Jim Rice in left field had hit .324 with 20 home runs; and Don Baylor, the team's DH, who swatted 31 home runs. They also had at first base former National League star Bill Buckner, who offered a solid bat for the Beantown lineup.

Pitching, a long-standing Boston weakness, also carried the team in the 1986 season. The Red Sox had AL Cy Young winner Roger Clemens. Clemens compiled a 24–4 season with 238 strikeouts in 254 innings. Bruce Hurst won 13 games and posted a 2.99 ERA, and "Oil Can" Boyd added 16 wins to the Boston cause. There was one member of the Boston pitching staff the Mets and their fans knew well, Tom Seaver. Seaver had joined the Red Sox during the season in a trade with the White Sox. The forty-one-year-old Seaver pitched well for Boston but a knee injury would force the future Hall of Famer to be a spectator in the Fall Classic.

The Series opened at Shea Stadium on Saturday October 18, 1986. Bruce Hurst took the mound for the Red Sox and the Mets countered with Ron Darling. Hurst was masterful, as was Darling but the Red Sox picked up a run in the sixth inning on an error by Tim Teufel. Ex-Met Calvin Schiraldi came on in relief for Hurst in the ninth and put down the Mets, giving the Red Sox a one-game advantage.

The Mets hoped to come back with Dwight Gooden in Game Two but it wouldn't be an easy task. Mets hitters were to battle

Roger Clemens. A pitchers' duel looked like it was on tap, but it never materialized.

The Red Sox reached Gooden for eight hits and six runs in five innings. By the end of the fifth inning Clemens was gone as well as the Mets had hit him for three runs. The final was 9–3 Boston and with the next three games scheduled for Fenway Park, hope was beginning to fade for the Mets.

Manager Davey Johnson decided to go with former Red Sox hurler Bobby Ojeda to start Game Three. The left-handed Ojeda put down the Red Sox 7–1. Lenny Dykstra led off the game for the Mets with a home run in the first inning. The Mets added three more runs and set the tone for Game Three. McDowell came on in relief of Ojeda in the eighth inning and secured the Mets win.

The Mets evened the Series in Game Four as they took advantage of fine pitching from Ron Darling, who pitched seven scoreless innings. Mets bats also came alive as Gary Carter poled two home runs and Lenny Dykstra hit his second home run of the series. Jesse Orosco notched a save and the Mets won 6–2.

With the series tied, the Red Sox went with Bruce Hurst, who had pitched so brilliantly in the opener at Shea. The Red Sox hoped for a similar performance in the final game at Fenway. The Mets went with their young ace Dwight Gooden, hoping for a better performance from their young star than shown in Game Two. But once again, Gooden disappointed, giving up nine hits and four runs in less than five innings. Hurst once again pitched well; he went the distance in the 4–2 Boston win. The Mets once again had their backs to the wall as the Series returned to New York. Hoping to rebound in Game Six of the 1986 World Series, the game would go down in storied annals as one of the greatest World Series games ever played.

Twenty-seven outs, that was all the Red Sox needed to win their first World Series since 1918. They had come close before in

1946, 1967, and 1975, but the folks in Beantown began to think that 1986 was finally their year.

The pitching matchup for Game Six was Bob Ojeda taking on Roger Clemens. The Red Sox got to Ojeda early scoring runs in the first and second innings. Clemens was pitching a no-hitter going into the fifth inning, when the Mets erupted for two runs to tie the score on key hits by Ray Knight and Mookie Wilson.

The Red Sox came back for a run in the seventh inning on a throwing error by Knight. Calvin Schiraldi came in for relief of Clemens in the eighth inning. Lee Mazzilli led the inning off with a single and took second on a successful bunt by Lenny Dykstra. Wally Backman sacrificed the runners over and Keith Hernandez walked, loading the bases. Gary Carter hit a sacrifice fly out to Jim Rice in left field, bringing Mazzilli in with the tying run.

The game went into extra innings and the Red Sox tried to end the game in the tenth inning and take the World Series. With Rick Aguilera on the mound, outfielder Dave Henderson sent a pitch over the wall, giving the Red Sox a 4–3 lead. Boston added another run that inning and took a 5–3 lead in the bottom of the tenth. The Red Sox were three outs away from their first championship in sixty-eight years.

Schiraldi put down the first two Mets in the tenth inning, Wally Backman flied to left and Keith Hernandez flied to center. The Red Sox were now only one out away. As Schiraldi faced Carter, for what the Red Sox hoped would be the final out, Red Sox players began standing on the dugout steps, ready to charge the field in celebration after the final out. Even the Shea Stadium scoreboard flashed the message, "CONGRATULATIONS, RED SOX."

But Carter sliced a Schiraldi pitch to left for a single. Kevin Mitchell stepped up to bat for Aguilera and lined to center for another single. Pandemonium was beginning to reign at Shea as the Mets mounted their rally.

With Carter on second, and Mitchell on first, the heroics continued when Ray Knight hit another single to center that scored Carter and moved Mitchell to third.

Boston manager John McNamara brought in Bob Stanley to face Mookie Wilson and put out the Mets' rally.

Wilson worked the count to 2–2 and then fouled off Stanley's next two pitches.

Stanley went with a fastball hoping to end the game, but it tailed toward Wilson who jumped away as Red Sox catcher Rick Gedman vainly tried to corral the ball but the pitch got past him and rolled all the way to the screen. Mitchell came home to tie the game and Ray Knight moved into scoring position at second.

After fouling off two more Stanley pitches, Wilson made contact and grounded a ball that trickled down the first-base line. Red Sox first baseman Bill Buckner got his glove down but not low enough—the ball went under Buckner's glove. Ray Knight came across home plate with the winning run for a 6–5 Mets victory and a game baseball fans will remember through the ages.

Game Seven seemed anticlimatic after the heroics of Game Six. The 1986 World Series boiled down to this last game, postponed for a day because of rain, allowing Mets fans an extra day to reflect on the glories of Game Six and Boston backers to lament the fate of their team.

The Red Sox scored three runs off of Ron Darling in the third inning, with outfielder Dwight Evans and catcher Rich Gedman blasting home runs. Wade Boggs knocked in another run with a single.

Sid Fernandez came on in relief for Darling in the fourth inning and put the Red Sox down through the sixth when the Mets came back.

Boston starter Bruce Hurst was still on the mound. With the bases loaded Hurst faced Keith Hernandez, who brought in two runs with a single. Wally Backman tied the game as he scooted home on a force play. The Mets were back in business.

New York picked up three more runs in the bottom of the seventh inning with Schiraldi in relief for Hurst. Knight led off with a home run. Hits by Lenny Dykstra and Rafael Santana and a sacrifice fly by Keith Hernandez brought in two more runs. After seven innings the score stood 6–3 Mets.

The Red Sox battled back in the eighth inning with two runs, but the Mets got an insurance run when Darryl Strawberry blasted a massive homer in the bottom of the inning.

The Mets added another run for good measure with a base hit by Jesse Orosco who had come into the game in the eighth inning.

Orosco registered twenty-one saves during the season and the Mets now needed three more outs from him.

Orosco went to work, striking out the first two Red Sox batters with ease. Then came second baseman Marty Barrett who collected thirteen hits during the Series. But Orosco was up to the challenge and struck Barrett out. The Mets won the World Championship.

The Mets celebrated their victory grandly. Ray Knight, who had almost been the goat in Game Six for his throwing error that allowed Boston to go ahead with what appeared to be the series-winning run, was voted Series MVP.

New York thanked the Mets with a parade down lower Broadway that culminated with festivities at City Hall. It had been a wonderful 25th season for the Mets and their fans.

CLOSE BUT NO CIGAR

The following season the Mets hoped for a repeat of their success in 1986, but injuries and other problems decimated their fine pitching staff. Mets pitchers spent a combined 457 days on the disabled list. Dwight Gooden was lost for two months because of cocaine abuse and ace reliever Roger McDowell was also lost for two months because of hernia problems. Despite the injuries, the Mets battled the St. Louis Cardinals for the league title up until the last week of the season. They finished three games behind the Cards, with 96 wins. In a record year for home runs, the Mets also had great offensive heroes. Darryl Strawberry and Howard Johnson became the first pair of 30–30 men in big league history. Strawberry belted 39 home runs and stole 36 bases. Howard Johnson landed 36 round trips and 32 stolen bases. Lenny Dykstra tied the club record of 37 doubles in a season and stole three bases in a game against the Expos on August first. Keith Hernandez won his tenth consecutive Gold Glove. The Mets first baseman hit a respectable .290 and the newly-acquired Kevin McReynolds, who came to the Mets in a trade during the off-season, played solidly in left field. McReynolds hit .276 with 29 home runs.

Despite injuries and Gooden's drug problems the Mets nonetheless sported five pitchers with double-digit winning records. And after missing the first two months of the season, Dwight Gooden came back strong finishing the year with 15 wins against 7 losses. Other double-digit winners were Ron Darling and Sid Fernandez, with 12 wins each, and Rick Aguilera and Terry Leach each with 11.

There was no doubt among Mets fans that with a healthy pitching staff the Mets would have easily repeated as NL East Champs.

Mets fans knew that with a sound pitching staff and their offensive muscle, a World Series appearance in 1988 was very likely. And it was. The Mets ran away with the NL East in 1988, finishing 15 games ahead of the second-place Pittsburgh Pirates.

Mets hitters tailed off in the second half of the season, but pitching, a longstanding Met strength carried the team.

Right-hander David Cone was superb in his second season with the team. The Kansas City native accounted for 20 wins against 3 losses with a cool 2.22 ERA. Doc Gooden pitched a full season and finished with an 18–9 record and Ron Darling was right behind him with 17 wins. The Mets pitching staff had the best ERA in the National League, with a combined 2.91 ERA. They also lead the league in strikeouts with 1,100.

On offense, Darryl Strawberry lead the NL with 39 round trippers and McReynolds knocked in 99 runs with 27 homers, a .288 average, and a steady, if not flashy, game in left field.

During the season Gary Carter blasted home run number 300. Shortstop Kevin Elster set a then-NL record for playing 60 games without an error, and, in an injury-plagued season, Howard Johnson still managed to hit 24 home runs. The much heralded rookie, Gregg Jefferies, joined the team in September and hit .321 with 6 home runs, living up to his minor league press clippings.

The New York fans appreciated their team's efforts as the Mets drew an all-time attendence record of 3,047,724.

The Los Angeles Dodgers would be the Mets' opponent in the National League Championship Series. If anything, the Mets were a confident lot, having taken the Dodgers in ten of eleven contests during the 1988 regular season. Unfortunately, the playoffs would be another story. The Dodgers won the NL West by seven games, but their lineup didn't throw fear into many pitchers' hearts.

The Dodgers' leader on the field was the hard-charging outfielder and former Michigan grid-iron hero, Kirk Gibson. The Dodger lineup also included Alfredo Griffin at shortstop, who hit only .199 during the season and first baseman John Shelby, who hit .223 with eight home runs. No one in the Dodger lineup hit more than .290 or had more than 25 home runs, except for Gibson.

Pitching was the strength of this Dodgers' team. They had three starting pitchers whose ERAs were less than 3.00. Orel Hershiser won 23 games with an ERA of 2.28; Tim Leary won 17 games with an ERA of 2.91; and Tim Belcher won 12 games and matched Leary's 2.91 ERA.

THE 1988 NATIONAL LEAGUE CHAMPIONSHIP SERIES

The series began in Los Angeles with Doc Gooden squaring off against Orel Hershiser. As dominant an opponent as Mike Scott had been in the 1986 NLCS, Hershiser proved to be just as potent. The Dodgers hurler ended the 1988 regular season with 59 consecutive innings without yielding a run. The Dodgers took a 2–0 lead in the ninth inning. Hershiser's streak rose to 67 innings, when the Mets scored two runs off a pop fly. The ball bounced off outfielder John Shelby's glove, allowing Darryl Strawberry to score the tying run and Kevin McReynolds to bowl over catcher Mike Scoscia with the winning run. Randy Myers, who came in for Gooden in the eighth inning, got the win.

The Dodgers tied the series up in Game Two as pitcher Tim Belcher singled with two outs in the second inning to ignite a four-run Dodger rally. Belcher struck out ten Mets and evened the series. Bad weather greeted the Mets and Dodgers as the series moved back to New York. Game Three was initially rained out and then played in a steady downpour the following day. The Dodgers went with Orel Hershiser to pitch and the Mets countered with Ron Darling.

The Dodgers took a 4–3 lead into the bottom of the eighth inning, but the Mets came through for five runs. Randy Myers, who came in for Roger McDowell in the eighth inning, got the win. Orlando Pena, who came in for Hershiser in the eighth inning, was tacked with the loss. The Mets took a 2–1 lead in the series.

The Dodgers showed muscle and grit in Game Four as Mike Scoscia belted a home run in the ninth inning that tied the game at four, and Kirk Gibson ended the game with a blast over the fence in the 12th inning, making the score 5–4 L.A. In Game Five, Hershiser, who had pitched seven innings the game before, came on in relief for the Dodgers in the twelfth inning, facing the Mets who had loaded the bases. The Dodger ace shut the door on the Mets, giving the Dodgers a 3–2 series advantage.

The Mets bounced back in Game Six, thanks to the efforts of pitcher David Cone who gave up five hits and one run as the Mets triumphed 5–1.

Kevin McReynolds was the hitting star with four hits. Once again the game went down to the wire.

Orel Hershiser took the mound for the Dodgers and pitched them to the World Series Championship. Hershiser shutout the Mets on five hits, not allowing a hit after the fourth inning. There was a celebration in L.A. but mourning in New York as most Mets fans concluded the better team had finished second.

The Dodgers went on to beat the Oakland A's in the World Series four games to one.

The Mets dreams of a dynasty began to fade in the injury-plagued 1989 season. Keith Hernandez suffered a broken knee-cap and missed two months of the season and finished the year hitting .233. The Mets first baseman was not resigned after the season. Hernandez signed with Cleveland but played sparingly, hitting a meager .200 and was out of baseball by 1991. Gary Carter was disabled in May and underwent knee surgery rendering him lost for the year. Injuries also befell the pitching staff as Dwight Gooden tore his right shoulder and was lost for most of the second half of the season.

Despite the crippling injuries the Mets finished second with a respectable 87–75 record, six games behind the NL East champs the Chicago Cubs. Third baseman Howard Johnson stole 41 bases and belted 36 home runs during the season as well as knocking in 101 runs. Darryl Strawberry hit 29 home runs but his batting average was .225, his lowest as a Met. During the season outfielder Mark Carreon tied a major league mark with four pinch-hit home runs.

The Mets pitching was consistent during the 1989 season,

with Sid Fernandez, David Cone, and Ron Darling tying for the team lead of 14 wins apiece. In the bullpen, Randy Myers saved 24 games, but was traded to Cincinnati in the off-season for Brooklyn native John Franco.

Many familiar faces were gone from the Mets lineup in 1989. Mookie Wilson was traded to Toronto for pitcher Jeff Musselman and Wally Backman was sent to Minnesota for three minor lea-guers. The second base spot opened up for the heralded Gregg Jefferies, who failed miserably at the position and hit .258, far from the promise he had showed in the last month and a half of the 1988 season.

In another trade with Minnesota, the Mets acquired Twins pitching ace Frank Viola for pitchers Rick Aguilera, Dave West, Kevin Tapani, and two minor league prospects.

The Mets got infielder/outfielder Juan Samuel from the Phillies for Lenny Dykstra and reliever Roger McDowell. Samuel was a bust as a Met and at season's end was traded to L.A. for power-hitting first baseman Mark Marshall and pitcher Alejandro Peña.

The Mets were retooling for the future with new players. Most of the heroes of 1986 were gone. On Opening Day 1990 Darryl Strawberry was the lone starter remaining from the 1986 Champi-onship team.

THE NINETIES

The Mets struggled early in the 1990 season. Mets management decided the way to remedy the situation was to fire their manger. On May 29 in Cincinnati, Davey Johnson was given his walking papers. Many Mets fans grumbled because it had been under Johnson's tutelage that the Mets captured a championship less than four years earlier and had come within a game of going back to the World Series in 1988. Johnson had also been the first manager in major league history to guide his team to five consecutive 90-game wins in a season.

Johnson's replacement was no stranger to Mets fans or players. The Mets elevated coach Bud Harrelson. Harrelson, the popular shortstop for the Mets from 1965–1977, had been a Mets coach since 1985.

The change seemed to perk up the Mets and stirred individual players to career performances. The Mets rode an 11 game winning streak from mid- to late June. Under Harrelson the team had a 71–49 record. The Mets ended the season in second place, four games behind NL East Champions the Pittsburgh Pirates.

During the season a number of Mets players set career records. David Cone recorded 233 K's, leading the NL in strikeouts. Frank Viola, in his first full season with the Mets, rang up 20 wins, the eighteenth pitcher to have 20 wins in both the AL and NL. Sid Fernandez finished the season with a losing record of 9–14 but NL hitters only put up a .200 batting average against the southpaw. Gooden finished with 19 wins against 7 losses and finished strong in September going 5–0. He was named NL Pitcher of the Month. John Franco led the NL with 33 saves. Mets batsmen also put up good numbers.

Catcher Mackey Sasser was hitting a torrid .336 at the All-Star break, but sprained his ankle and never returned to form, though he still ended the season hitting a credible .307. First baseman Dave Magadan hit NL pitching at a .328 clip, but showed little pop in his swing with only 6 home runs. Kevin McReynolds played his usual steady, if unspectacular, game in left field, contributing 24 round trippers to the Mets cause in the 1990 season, his fifth consecutive season of belting 20 or more home runs.

Ironically Darryl Strawberry had his career year in 1990, hitting 37 home runs with 108 RBIs. Strawberry decided to pack it in with the Mets and signed with the Dodgers for $23.5 million. Mets fans knew an era had ended. They lamented and held their breath and waited with some apprehension for this new era to begin.

The new era began in 1991 when, after finishing first or second for the previous seven years, the Mets fell to fifth in the NL East 20½ games behind the first-place Pittsburgh Pirates.

Manager Bud Harrelson was fired toward the tail-end of the season and replaced with third base coach Mike Cubbage, whose stint as a Mets manger was the shortest in Mets history. Cubbage finished the season posting a 3–4 record.

Harrelson's failings, beside the team's mediocre performance on the field, included his bickering with the media over many of his managerial decisions, dissension in the clubhouse, and a blowup with ace pitcher David Cone. With a week left in the season, Harrelson was history.

Despite the fifth-place finish some Mets were still showing a lot of hustle. Howard Johnson, who during the season had stints at third base, shortstop, and the outfield, brought in 117 RBIs and led the NL in home runs with 38. David Cone, despite getting little support from a struggling Mets lineup, won 14 games and led the NL in strikeouts for a second straight year with 241.

Cone saved his best effort for the last game of the 1991 season with a 19-strikeout outing against the Phillies on the last day of the 1991 season.

Injuries dogged the Mets during the 1991 season. In the off-season, after Strawberry departed for LA, the Mets decided a new look was needed to replace the departed slugger.

The Mets went for speed, picking up Vince Coleman from the Cardinals. Coleman had stolen 519 bases his first six seasons in the major leagues. The Mets expected similar numbers from the twenty-nine-year-old outfielder.

Coleman played only 72 games in the 1991 season due to assorted injuries. He hit .255 and, despite his limited playing time, proved he had not lost any of his base-stealing skill. He led the Mets with 37 swipes.

But there were other disappointments for the 1991 Mets. Pitcher Frank Viola, who posted a 10–5 mark at the All-Star break, ended the season with only a 13–15 record that included seven consecutive losses.

The Mets went on a tear in July winning ten straight games in the middle of the month, but in August their fortunes went south and they lost eleven straight. It was a season of peaks and a lot of valleys. Once again the Mets realized changes were needed to lift this team out of the mire and back into contention. During the season Ron Darling, a mainstay of the 1986 pitching staff, was dealt to Montreal for reliever Tim Burke.

Jeff Torborg was lured from Chicago to return to New York to manage. Torborg, a Jersey native, had only a marginal career in the big leagues catching for the Dodgers and Angels, but could claim the amazing feat of having caught no-hitters for Sandy Koufax, Bill Singer, and Nolan Ryan. After his playing days were over he managed the Indians from 1977–1979. He then spent ten years in the Bronx as a Yankees coach before joining the White Sox.

Torborg took over the floundering White Sox and three seasons later they were a strong contending team in the American League. It was expected that he would be able to do the same with the Mets.

Money didn't seem much of an object as the Mets took out their checkbooks and signed outfielder Bobby Bonilla from Pittsburgh, and first baseman Eddie Murray from the Dodgers. The Mets hoped that the hard-hitting duo would add punch to their weak lineup.

The pitching staff was overhauled as well. The Mets lost pitcher Frank Viola to the Red Sox through free agency, but two-time Cy Young winner Bret Saberhagen was brought in as a replacement. The twenty-eight-year-old right-hander came to the Mets in a trade that also brought over utility infielder Bill Pecota for Kevin McReynolds, Gregg Jefferies, and infielder Keith Miller. With the added firepower and Saberhagen on the mound, the Mets were considered to be a top contender for the NL East in 1992.

Injuries dampened the Mets dreams in 1992 as the team once again stumbled into a second straight fifth-place finish with a 72–90 mark, twenty-four games behind the NL East champion Pittsburgh Pirates. Fourteen Mets went on the disabled list during the season, the most notable being Bret Saberhagen. In the season starter against the Dodgers, Saberhagen came out of the game in the fifth inning complaining of tendinitis in his pitching hand. The injury side-lined him for the rest of the season. The former Cy Young Award winner finished the season with a record of only 3–5.

Other players who joined Saberhagen on the DL were starters Howard Johnson, Dave Magadan, and the newly acquired Willie Randolph. Vince Coleman was also plagued by injuries and only managed to steal twenty-four bases during the season.

In the tail-end of the season the Mets traded David Cone to Toronto for outfielder Ryan Thompson and second baseman Jeff Kent, two young prospects with great promise.

Eddie Murray, in the twilight of his Hall of Fame career, knocked in 93 RBIs, hit 16 home runs, but hit only .261. Bobby Bonilla, who the Mets and their fans thought should be in his prime at twenty-nine batted only .249, with 19 home runs, numbers far lower than those he had produced previously for the Pirates.

With David Cone gone to Canada, Sid Fernandez was the Mets top pitcher with 14 wins. Dwight Gooden ended the year with a 10–13 record and John Franco, fighting elbow problems, picked up only 15 saves as the Mets top reliever.

Mets fans hoped their heroes would get healthy in 1993 and that the team would explode into contention. There would be explosions, but not all of them on the field in 1993.

The Mets came in dead last in 1993, losing 103 games. Even the expansion Florida Marlins finished five games better than them. The Mets had the lowest team batting average in the NL with a sorry .248. Jeff Torborg was replaced in mid-May with Dallas Green.

The six-foot-five-inch Green had a reputation for speaking his mind but he had managed the Phillies to a championship in 1980. Two decades earlier he had pitched as a spot starter and reliever for the Phillies. He left Philadelphia in 1981 to become the GM for the Chicago Cubs. Green held the job for nearly six seasons and helped build the Cubs into a team that made it to the 1984 World Series. Green left Chicago in 1987 citing "philosophical differences" with team owners.

George Steinbrenner signed Green to manage the Yankees in 1989, but fired him in mid-August.

Green did a little better than Torborg. Despite the efforts of Bobby Bonilla, who slugged a career high 34 home runs, and an aging Eddie Murray, who contributed 100 RBIs, there was little bang for the buck in the Mets lineup.

Bret Saberhagen, still battling injuries, was shelved in early August though he did show some bang off the field when he threw a firecracker at a group of reporters; he showed little on the mound with another dismal, injury-shortened season.

Vince Coleman had another disappointing season as a Met that year as well. Coleman caused an explosion off the field when he threw a firecracker out of his car window after a game at Dodgers Stadium, injuring a woman and two small children. He was charged with a felony, and the team placed him on "administrative leave" for the remainder of the season.

Coleman's destructive antics were not just aimed at fans. In April 1994 Coleman swung his golf club in the Mets clubhouse and injured Doc Gooden. In 1994 he was sent to Kansas City and would finish his career with the Royals in 1996.

A record was set in 1993 by pitcher Anthony Young, who lost twenty-seven straight decisions. The reliever and spot starter finished with a 1–16 record in 1993.

Eddie Murray left the Mets, signing on with the Cleveland Indians (and returned to the AL).

With one less bat in the lineup, few expected much for the 1994 season.

The Mets began to rise during 1994. The short season ended with a strike on August 11. The Mets finished third in the NL East, 18 and a half games behind the first-place Montreal Expos. The Mets totaled 55 wins and 58 losses, a 20-and-a-half-game pickup from 1993.

Bret Saberhagen finally reached the promise the Mets had hoped for when they tapped him from Kansas City two seasons earlier. Saberhagen finished with a 14–4 record an ERA of 2.74. He also set a modern day baseball record of 0.7 walks per nine innings pitched. During the 1994 Saberhagen put together a walkless streak of 47.1 innings.

Other notable pitching accomplishments were Bobby Jones' mark of 12–7 with a 3.15 ERA, and John Franco, one of the top fireman in the NL, scored 30 saves. Second baseman Jeff Kent led Mets hitters with a .292 average and Bonilla provided the team with power, smacking in 20 home runs.

One sad note in the 1994 season was Doc Gooden's continuing problems with drugs. Once the golden boy of the New York Mets, Gooden managed only three wins during the season before being placed on suspension by the league for his substance abuse. This suspension effectively ended his career with the Mets.

Gooden would retire from baseball in 2001, never approaching, the potential he had shown in his first two season with the Mets.

The 1995 season began late due to the players' stike that had curtailed the previous season. The Mets finished the 1995 season in second place with a 69–75 record, 20 games behind NL East Champs the Atlanta Braves. The Mets put together a 44–31 record after the All-Star break, finishing strong down the stretch.

First baseman Rico Brogna was the top Mets power hitter with 22 home runs and 76 RBIs. Brett Butler, the thirty-eight-year-old center fielder, hit .311 and stole 21 bases before being dealt back to the Los Angeles Dodgers.

Bobby Bonilla, another established star, garnered an impressive .325 batting average with 18 home runs, but by the end of the season the thirty-two-year-old Bronx native was dealt to the Baltimore Orioles for outfielders Alex Ocha and Damon Buford.

The Mets, however, were not finished making trades. On July 31, Bret Saberhagen, whose record stood at 5–5, was sent to the Colorado Rockies for minor league pitchers Juan Acevedo and Arnold Gooch.

With Saberhagen gone the Mets ace pitcher became Bobby Jones, who posted a 10–10 record and an 4.19 ERA, nothing that would make Mets fans forget Tom Seaver or Dwight Gooden. A bright glimmer of hope for the struggling pitching staff was rookie Jason Isringhausen, who finished the season with a 9–2 record, a 2.81 ERA, and received some consideration for NL Rookie of the Year. John Franco was his dependable self, saving twenty-nine games and posting his eighth season of 20 or more saved games. Mets fans found little solace in the team's second-place finish. Some questioned if Dallas Green was the right guy for the job of managing the Mets. In mid-November the Mets announced they had signed Bobby Valentine to manage the Norfolk Tides, their top minor league team. It was Valentine's second time around with the Tides. The aggressive, outspoken Valentine was no stranger to the Mets uniform and rumors started Valentine would be at Shea before the end of the 1996 season.

There were offensive fireworks at Shea during the 1996 season. Catcher Todd Hundley cranked out 41 home runs during the season and knocked in 112 runs. Hundley wasn't the only power guy in the lineup; his mark of 112 RBIs was bested by Bernard Gilkey, who had 117 RBIs. Gilkey was acquired by the Mets from the Cardinals for a contingent of prospects. The former Cardinals outfielder did it all hitting a potent .317 with 30 home runs and placing among the league leaders in RBIs. Gilkey and Hundley were the first two Mets to go over 100 RBIs in the same season. Lance Johnson, picked up from the White Sox via the free agency route, gave the Mets the leadoff threat they had lacked in the past few seasons. With a .333 batting average, Johnson was often on base and frequently stole the next one. The outfielder stole 50 bases during the '96 season, threatening Mookie Wilson's Met record of 58 in a season. Johnson also tallied 227 hits, the highest total in the NL history since Pete Rose's 230 hits in 1973.

Pitching even perked up a bit as Mark Clark, obtained from the Cleveland Indians in late March for outfielder Ryan Thompson and pitcher Reid Cornelius, scored a respectable ERA of 3.43. Jason Isringhausen, who showed so much promise in the second half of his rookie season in 1995, was bothered by a tear in his pitching shoulder and bone chips, which were removed in an operation at the tail-end of the season. The promising Isringhausen slumped to 6–14. Bobby Jones added a dozen victories to the Mets cause in 1996, improving his win mark by two over the previous season. Despite the impressive offense in 1996 and the improved pitching staff, the Mets could win no more than 71 games and ended up losing 91. They finished fourth in the NL East, twenty-five games behind the Atlanta Braves who won the NL East pennant for a third consecutive year.

Dallas Green was fired in September and, as most expected, Bobby Valentine was named the sixteenth Mets manager since the team first took the field in 1962. Mets fans awaited the start of the 1997 to see what the brash Valentine would do for the Mets in the coming season.

THE VALENTINE MAGIC AND TURMOIL

The Mets turned it around in 1997, winning 88 games and losing 74. Valentine and the Mets produced the first winning season at Shea Stadium since 1990 and showed an improvement of 17 games in the standings from 1996.

The Mets took on the aggressive "never say die" spirit of their manager. Along with the Atlanta Braves, the Mets enjoyed the best home record in the National League at 50–31. Todd Hundley whacked 30 home runs, first baseman John Olerud, who the Mets picked up from Toronto in late 1996 for pitcher Robert Person, paid off handsomely, driving in 102 runs, Butch Huskey, who alternated his playing time between third base, first base, and the outfield, swatted 24 home runs. The twenty-three-year-old Edgardo Alfonzo started his first full season with the Mets at third base and hit a .315 average with 10 home runs. Bobby Jones picked up 15 wins during the season. The Mets top winner, Rick Reed, posted 13 wins in his first full season in the majors at the advanced age of 32. Reed also had a ERA average of 2.85, the best of any pitcher in the starting rotation. The big story on the pitching staff was John Franco, whose 36 saves made him the National League's all-time save leader.

Perhaps the biggest highlight of the 1997 season occured on June 16 when the Mets and Yankees faced off at Yankee Stadium. This was the first time since the Dodgers and the Giants left New York that two New York teams squared off. This superhyped series between crosstown rivals brought back memories of the old Subway Series between the Dodgers and the Yankees in the 1950s.

The Mets were on the upswing, many felt the improvement was due to their fiery leader Bobby Valentine. Valentine however was not without his detractors, most notably pitcher Pete Harnisch and outfielder Lance Johnson. Both players approached Valentine over playing time and, in Harnisch's case, remarks that Valentine allegedly made about the right-hander's battle with depression. Ugly confrontations arose, Harnisch was given his release, but was later picked up by the Brewers.

Lance Johnson was dealt to the Cubs. The Mets appeared to have turned the corner in 1998 and were a contending team once again. One thing was sure, the Mets were not going to be boring with Bobby Valentine in the dugout.

They came within a game of going to the playoffs, but it was a painful final week as the Mets lost their final five games and blew any chance for postseason play. When the season ended the Mets stood at 88–74, the same record they had in 1997.

The big story for the Mets during 1998 was the acquisition of megastar Mike Piazza. The future Hall of Famer, who some consider the greatest hitting catcher of all time, came to the Mets in a trade that sent top prospect outfielder Preston Wilson and minor league pitchers Ed Yarnell and Geoff Goetz to the Florida Marlins.

Piazza started the season with the Dodgers, where he had played the previous six season and had put up awesome hitting numbers. Fans viewed the acquisition as perhaps the biggest in the history of the club.

With Piazza behind the plate the Mets now had to do something about their other heavy-hitting catcher Todd Hundley, who was hobbled in 1998 by a shoulder injury. He tried playing the outfield without great success and a rift developed between Hundley and the Mets over an alleged drinking problem that had been leaked to the press by "unnamed sources" in the Mets front office. Bobby Valentine added fuel to the fire when he mentioned that Hundley needed more sleep. Many in the media felt the irascible Valentine was alluding to the alleged alcohol problem. In the off-season Todd Hundley was dealt to the Dodgers for outfielder Roger Cedeño and catcher Charles Johnson.

Mike Piazza played in 109 games for the Mets, hit a sizzling .345 and topped the team in home runs with 23.

The surprise story of the year was first baseman John Olerud who hit .354 and was one home run behind Piazza with 22. The infield play was solid with Carlos Baerga at second, the slick fielding Rey Ordoñez at shortstop and Edgardo Alfonzo at third. Alfonzo continued to hit with a steady .278 batting average and 17 home runs.

Al Leiter posted 17 wins against only 6 losses and had an impressive ERA of 2.45. Right-hander Rick Reed gave the Mets a potent one–two punch on the mound, winning 16 games and posting an ERA of 3.48. Behind the lefty-righty duo of Leiter and Reed other Mets pitchers who worked the starting rotation could only contribute 26 wins. The thirty-seven-year-old John Franco continued to amaze and place his name in the record books. During the season Franco posted his 397th save for a number-two ranking on the all-time save list and on June 16 he passed Tom Seaver for most games pitched in as a Met with 402.

Two oddities took place at Shea Stadium during the season. The Mets took the field to play the Phillies on March 31, the earliest season opener for the Mets, with the temperature reaching 88 degrees in a game that went 14 innings. The Mets finally won. And on April 15 the Mets and Yankees shared Shea Stadium for a day because of repair work being done on Yankees Stadium. The Mets beat the Cubs 2–1 and the Yankees bested the California Angels 6–3. It was a memorable day in New York baseball.

The Mets knocked on the playoff door in the 1998 season but stumbled badly in the last week. With Mike Piazza in the lineup on the starting day in 1999, the Mets were ready to batter down the door.

The Mets did batter down the door, but it wasn't easy. Despite finishing the season with a 97–65 record the Mets had to play the Cincinnati Reds in a one-game playoff to determine the wild-card spot in the NL.

Thanks to the strong left arm of Al Leiter the Mets prevailed. Leiter pitched a two-hitter, shutting out the Reds. The Mets then bested the new kids on the NL block, the Arizona Diamondbacks.

The expansion team was only in its second season, but, because of free agency their roster was dotted with established stars. The Diamondbacks won 100 games during that season, an unheard of mark for a team in their second year. The Mets rocked

Arizona's ace and NL Cy Young Award winner Randy Johnson in Game One thanks to two home runs by Edgardo Alfonzo. The final score was 8–4 Mets.

Arizona got their split in Game Two as they took the Mets and Kenny Rogers 7–1. The game was decided when Arizona jumped on Kenny Rogers for three runs in the third inning.

The Mets ended the best-of-five series at Shea where the Mets pounded the Diamondbacks for 11 hits and nine runs in Game Three to win 9–2. Arizona held a 3–2 lead going into the bottom of the eighth when Diamondbacks' outfielder Tony Womack dropped a fly ball that allowed the Mets to tie the game at three.

Todd Pratt ended the game in the bottom of the tenth as he put a Matt Mantei pitch over the fence. Pratt, the Mets' second-string catcher had become an unlikely series hero.

The Mets celebration was short-lived because they now had to face the perpetual NL East Champion Atlanta Braves in the League Championship Series.

The Braves, under manager Bobby Cox, won 103 games during the regular season. They possessed a heavy-hitting team with five players who hit 20 or more home runs during the season. Atlanta's attack was paced by Larry "Chipper" Jones, the National League's MVP for 1999. Jones hit .319 with 45 home runs and knocked in 110 runs.

On the mound the Braves were sparked by future Hall of Famer Greg Maddux, who won 19 games during the season, and 24-year-old Kevin Millwood, who finished at 18–7 with a potent 2.68 ERA. John Rocker was a force to deal with coming out of the bullpen. Rocker saved 38 games during the season and was an excellent fireman.

Greg Maddux polished off the Mets in Game One with a five-hit seven-inning effort and a 4–2 Braves win. Masato Yoshii took the loss for the Mets. John Rocker came in in the eighth inning and shut the door on the Mets.

The trend continued in the next two games with Atlanta taking Game Two 4–3. The series left Atlanta and came to New York with the Braves in the driver's seat commanding a 2–0 lead.

Things didn't improve much at Shea for Game Three. The Braves shut out the Mets 1–0. Tom Glavine got the win for the Braves and Al Leiter, who had pitched a masterful game for seven innings, was tagged with the loss. The Mets had their backs up against the wall as they stood one game away from elimination.

The Mets displayed their no-quit attitude coming back in Game Four. The final was 4–3 Mets.

It took a grand slam "single" by Robin Ventura to give the Mets a 4–3 victory in the fifteenth inning of Game Five. Ventura's heroics were one of the most unusual in Met history. The third baseman smacked one out of Shea stadium with the bases full, but as Ventura was heading around the bases he was overtaken by his joyous teammates, who had charged the field. The umps ruled Ventura's blow a two-run single but few Mets fans complained. The Mets were coming back and some wondered if this was the year for the Subway Series and a shot at the Yankees, who would clinch the AL flag the following day in their championship series against the Red Sox.

Game Six would go down in the annals of Mets history as another unforgettable postseason game.

After falling behind 5–0 in the first inning and Al Leiter knocked out of the game, the Mets came back taking a 9–8 lead in the top of the eighth. The Braves battled back to tie the game at nine in the bottom half of the inning.

The Mets once again took the lead in their half of the tenth inning, but once again the Braves came back in their half of the inning and took the game in the bottom of the eleventh with Kenny Rogers walking in the winning run. Atlanta took the series 4–2 and would face the Yankees in the World Series.

Mets fans could take solace that their team had battled the

Braves in each game and lost by no more than one run in three of their four losses.

The Mets set a league record in 1999 for fewest errors in a season with 68. The infield also proved iron-clad allowing only 33 errors, also a league record. Rey Ordoñez finished the season setting an individual record by playing 100 consecutive games as a shortstop without an error.

The offense was potent as well. Mike Piazza blasted 40 home runs, and hit .303 with 124 RBIs. Ventura earned his paycheck playing solidly at third base, hitting .301 with 32 home runs and 120 RBIs. Second baseman Edgardo Alfonzo showed big-league crowds that he was one of the best hitting second baseman in the majors, posting a .304 average with 27 home runs, and 108 RBIs.

Al Leiter and Orel Hershiser were the Mets top starters with 13 wins each. In 1998 the Mets had knocked on the door, in 1999 they had battered it down, and in 2000 they would enter the house.

2000: A SUBWAY SERIES FOR A NEW MILLENNIUM

The year 2000 was the one that New York baseball fans had long been awaiting. It was the year when the Mets and the Yankees finally faced-off in the World Series. The Mets battled throughout the season, starting the year earlier than the 28 other major league teams who were still ending spring training back in the States. The Mets and the Chicago Cubs opened up the new season and the new millennium on the other side of the world in Japan. The Mets and Cubs split the two-game series at the Tokyo Dome and returned back to the States to get back to business.

The Mets were the favorite in the race to cop the National League pennant and they laid out their message early, going 16–10 in April. Mike Hampton had come to the Mets in a trade with the Houston Astros. Hampton had won 22 games in 1999 and had finished second in the Cy Young voting. The price for Hampton was not cheap. The Mets gave Houston outfielder Roger Cedeño, who had hit .313 and stolen 66 bases during the previous season and pitcher Octavio Dotel. John Olerud chose free agency at season's end and returned to his native Washington state to play for the Seattle Mariners.

With Olerud's departure there was a hole at first base. The Mets filled it with Todd Zeile from the Texas Rangers. The outfield had a new look as well. Journeyman Derek Bell, who had come to the Mets in the Hampton deal, was in left, Rookie Jay Payton was in center, and Benny Agbayani, Joe McEwing, and Rickey Henderson were platooned at right. Henderson had raised the ire of the Mets and the fans when he and Bobby Bonilla, who had rejoined the Mets for a second stint during 1999, contributed little more than a .180 batting average and also played cards in the clubhouse in the last innings of the final game of the NLCS. Bonilla was once again gone from the Mets. Henderson would start the 2000 season with the team, but would play poorly, and soon be released. Henderson later played for Seattle during 2000 and hit .238.

The Mets hung tough during the season, but never overtook their old nemesis, the Atlanta Braves. When all was said and done the Mets had fought Atlanta down to the wire but stumbled against the Braves in early September. They clinched a playoff spot in the last week of the season with a 6–2 win in a four-hit effort by Rick Reed over the Braves.

During the 2000 season Mike Piazza hit .324 tying for the team's best batting average with Edgardo Alfonzo. Piazza led the Mets in home runs with 38, including 3 grand slams. The Norristown, Pennsylvania, native also knocked in 124 runs. Todd Zeile was a welcome addition at first base after the departure of John Olerud. Zeile hit .288 with 22 home runs. Rookie Jay Payton played well in center field, hitting .291 with 17 home runs. The twenty-seven-year-old Payton was also a strong candidate for NL

Rookie of the Year. Second baseman Edgardo Alfonzo once again put up solid numbers and played a steady defensive game, and banged out 25 home runs on a solid .324 with 94 RBIs.

Al Leiter finished with 16 wins, one more than Mike Hampton who led the team in ERA with a 3.14. Armando Benitez set a Mets record with 41 saves. Glendon Rusch, who the Mets picked up from Kansas City late in the season, contributed 11 wins as he worked his way into the starting rotation. Leiter, Alfonzo, and Piazza were all named to the All-Star team, the most Mets since 1990. Leiter also won the Roberto Clemente Award, for skills and civic responsibility. The Mets once again clinched a wild-card playoff spot with five games to go in the 2000 season. They faced the San Francisco Giants in the Divisional Championship Series. The Giants ran away with the NL West, finishing 11 games ahead of the second-place Los Angeles Dodgers. Under manager Dusty Baker the Giants finished with a 97–65 mark. The Giants were paced by their slugger Barry Bonds, who walloped 49 home runs. The right fielder also hit .304 with 106 RBIs. Former Mets teammate Jeff Kent also added muscle to the Giants' offensive machine with a .334 average. The second baseman also led the team with a 125 RBIs and blasted 33 home runs.

On the mound the Giants had a nice right-left combo with Livan Hernandez and Shawn Estes. The duo combined for 32 wins during the season. Robb Nen was a force coming out of the bullpen as the Giants closer. Nen had 41 saves and iced NL hitters with a 1.50 ERA. The best-of-five series began on October 4 in San Francisco.

As they often did in the playoffs, the Mets bit the bullet in the first game. The Giants coasted to an easy 5–1 win. Bonds came through for the Giants with timely hitting and Ellis Burks blasted a three-run homer off starter Mike Hampton, who was tagged for the loss.

Down by one the Mets went back to work in Game Two taking

a 4–1 lead into the bottom of the ninth. The big break for the Mets was a two-run homer by Edgardo Alfonzo. But, their usually reliable closer, Benitez, gave it away in the ninth when J. T. Snow homered with Kent and Bonds on base, forcing the game into extra innings. The Mets took the game in the tenth inning when Jay Payton brought Darryl Hamilton home on a base hit off Felix Rodriguez. John Franco shut the Giants down in the bottom of the inning and evened the series.

Game Three moved back east to Shea Stadium. The Giants took a 2–0 lead in the fourth inning, but the Mets chipped away at the San Francisco lead. The game was tied 2–2 in the bottom of the eighth and would stay tied until the thirteenth inning when Benny Agbayani ended it with a blast off of Giants pitcher Aaron Fultz that sailed high over the left-field fence. The Mets took the series lead, needing just one more to move on to the NL Championship.

Bobby Jones the right-hander, not to be confused with Bobby M. Jones the left-hander of the Mets 2000 pitching ensemble, pitched the game of his life. He shut out the Giants yielding a lone hit, a Jeff Kent double in the fifth inning, and two walks. The Mets produced four runs during the game, two of them off a Robin Ventura home run in the first inning. But the hero of the day was Jones whom Bobby Valentine nearly didn't pitch.

The day before, the St. Louis Cardinals completed their rout of the Mets old nemesis the Atlanta Braves. The Mets would battle the Cards for the NL flag and a shot at the World Series.

The St. Louis Cardinals not only swept the Atlanta Braves in the divisional playoffs, but during the season had run roughshod over the NL Central Division, winning it by ten games. St. Louis finished with 95 wins, their high octane offense pounding out 235 home runs, 32 of them by slugger Mark McGwire, who due to a knee injury, appeared in fewer than half the regular season games. With McGwire on the bench the Cardinals offensive pop rested on the capable bats of Jim Edmonds, who had blasted 42 home runs and knocked in 108 runs, and former Met Ray Lankford, with 26 home runs.

The Cardinals' pitching staff was led by Darryl Kile who, along with Tom Glavine from the Braves, was the only National Leaguer to win 20 or more games during the 2000 season. Garret Stephenson, Pat Hentgen, and Andy Benes combined for another 43 wins in the starting rotation. The only left-hander was twenty-one-year-old Rick Ankiel, who put together a promising 11–7 season. The 2000 NLCS began October 11 in St. Louis with the Cards favored to take the series, but the Mets paid little attention to the odds.

Mike Hampton pitched a masterpiece in Game One, shutting out the Cards in the seven innings he pitched. John Franco came on in the eighth and Armando Benitez finished up in the ninth. The Mets took Game One 6–2 and were off and running.

The Mets continued to roll on to the World Series as they took Game Two 6–5, on Jay Payton's tie-breaking base hit in the top of the ninth. Turk Wendell, who had come on in the eighth inning, picked up the win and Rick Ankiel, who didn't last through the first inning because of wildness, took the loss.

Game Three was played at Shea Stadium on October 14 and, as some Mets fans began talking sweep, the Cardinals bounced back, shelling Rick Reed early, with eight hits and five runs in three innings. The Cards took the game 8–2 and tightened the series 2–1. In Game Four the Cards started Darryl Kile on three days' rest.

The Mets got to Kile at the onset, with a record-setting five doubles in the first inning. The Mets took the game 10–6 as Mike Piazza blasted his second homer of the series and little used outfielder Timo Perez woke up the Shea Stadium crowd. Perez, who had played for the Hiroshima Toyo Carp in the Japanese Central League the season before, had two hits and stole two bases in Game Four. Glendon Rusch picked up the win coming in for a struggling Bobby Jones in the fifth inning.

One more win and the Mets would be going to the World Series. New York prayed for a Subway Series. The Mets took the Cards 6–0 in Game Five winning the NL flag. Mike Hampton was once again invincible as he went the distance giving up just three hits to the Cards. Todd Zeile's base-clearing double in the fourth inning that made the score the final 6–0 took Cardinal starter Pat Hentgen out of the game.

The New York National League team had won it's fourth pennant and would be going to the Fall Classic for the first time since 1986. The Mets celebrated that night and waited to find out who would win the ALCS series. The following day the Yankees triumphed over Seattle 9–7. New Yorkers would get their first Subway Series since 1956.

BRING ON THE YANKEES

The ghosts of previous Fall Classics hung heavy over the Big Apple the week of the World Series. Ruth, Gehrig, DiMaggio, and Mantle wearing Yankee pinstripes and Jackie Robinson, Pee Wee Reese, and Roy Campanella the beloved bums of Flatbush were all there in spirit. One could see a huge smile beaming down from baseball heaven on the face of Charles Dillon Stengel.

There were new heroes in 2000. For the Yankees there was Derek Jeter, the charismatic shortstop who hit .339 during the season, and Bernie Williams, who was an All-Star center fielder who hit .307 and had 30 home runs.

On the mound the Mets would face Andy Pettitte, who had rang up 19 wins during the regular season and Roger Clemens, the future Hall of Famer who had stirred the wrath of the Mets when he beaned Mike Piazza during a regular season interleague game. The Clemens–Piazza row was just added drama to the already megahyped Series.

The 2000 World Series got under way on of October 21 at Yankee Stadium. The mound matchups were Al Leiter versus Andy Pettitte. A crowd of 57,545 took their seats as Billy Joel sang the National Anthem and were about to witness the longest game in the history of the World Series.

The Mets blew early opportunities as they put the lead man on in the second through sixth innings. It was the sixth inning that broke Mets fans hearts and set a negative tone for the rest of the Series.

With Timo Perez on first with two out, Zeile took a Pettitte pitch deep. Perez, thinking Zeile had homered, was not running hard until he saw the ball bounce off the wall to Yankees outfielder Dave Justice. Justice relayed to Yankee shortstop Derek Jeter, who nailed Perez at home for the final out of the inning.

Justice proved a thorn in the Mets' side throughout the game as he knocked in two runs with a double in the bottom of the inning. The Yankees took a 2–0 lead but the Mets wouldn't let that stick.

Bubba Trammel brought in two Mets runs with a pinch-hit single and Edgardo Alfonzo brought in another run with an infield single. The Mets had a 3–2 lead going into the ninth inning.

The Mets went to their closer to save the game.

Armando Benitez took the mound and prepared to close the door on the Yankees. Benitez got Jorge Posada to fly out to lead off the inning but then outfielder Paul O'Neill took first base on a walk. Luis Polonia sent O'Neill to second on a base hit, and up stepped Yankee second baseman Jose Vizcaino. The former Met had joined the Yankees during the season and had hit only .200 with men in scoring position. But that night he put an Armando Benitez fastball into left field to load the bases. Chuck Knoblauch, who was the Yankees' DH, brought in O'Neill with a sacrifice fly and put the game into extra innings. The Yankees' relief pitchers Jeff Nelson, Mariano Rivera, and Mike Stanton combined for over five innings of shutout ball. In the bottom of the thirteenth inning it would be Jose Vizcaino who would once again be the Yankees' hero and haunt the Mets.

With two outs in the bottom of the thirteenth Vizcaino singled home Tino Martinez off of Turk Wendell, who had come on in the eleventh inning and took the loss. The game ended after four hours and fifty-one minutes, the longest in the history of the World Series.

For Yankees fans it was worth the wait, but for Mets fans it was a painful loss. Many would lament the base running of Timo Perez in the sixth inning as a turning point in the Series.

The Yankees put Roger Clemens on the mound to face the Mets in Game Two. The crowd of 57,545 anticipated a face-off between Clemens and Piazza. They wouldn't have long to wait. Clemens had his game face on, mowing down the Mets with his 90-mile-an-hour-plus fastball that was still the scourge of the AL.

Timo Perez went down on a blazing fastball clocked at 97 miles an hour. Edgardo Alfonzo took a K from Clemens on a splitter, and up stepped Mike Piazza. With a one-ball, two-strike count, Clemens fired a fastball at Piazza which splintered the catcher's bat. The barrel of the bat went flying toward the mound and landed a few feet from Clemens, who picked it up and hurled it in the direction of Piazza, who was sprinting down the first-base line.

The Mets catcher took Clemens' gesture as hostile and headed toward the Yankees' pitcher but umpire Charlie Reliford restored order. Clemens would be fined by the commissioner's office for the bat-throwing incident. The fine was of little comfort to the Mets. Clemens was nearly flawless during his eight innings, striking out nine Mets, giving up two hits and walking none.

The Yankees had a 6–0 lead in the ninth inning as they brought on Jeff Nelson to relieve Clemens in a mop-up role.

The Mets rallied in the top of the ninth on a Mike Piazza blast that brought in two runs. But the final score was 6–5 as Mariano Rivera got Kurt Abbot to make the final out of the game.

The Yankees swept at home and their fans were realizing their dream of a "three-peat." For Mets fans, they hoped the team would rally back in Queens and the heroics of the ninth inning in the second game would breathe some life into their heroes.

Rick Reed and Orlando Hernandez took the mound in Game Three at Shea. With a 2–0 Yankee lead in the Series, the Mets had their backs against the wall, and the odds were running against them. Going into the third game of the 2000 World Series the Yankees had run a streak of 14 consecutive postseason victories and the pitcher that night, "El Duque," had an 8–0 record in his postseason career.

Both Reed and Hernandez battled the first six innings, with the Yankees holding on to a 2–1 lead. The Mets tied the game in the bottom of the sixth as Todd Zeile doubled into the left-field corner. Rick Reed came out after the sixth inning but "El Duque" continued to battle with the skill and guile that made him one of the AL's top hurlers, striking out 12 Mets, until the eighth when the Mets toppled "El Duque" and the Yankees.

Benny Agbayani took an "El Duque" fastball into the left-field gap, scoring Todd Zeile from first. Jay Payton moved Agbayani to third on an infield hit and pinch hitter Bubba Trammell brought him home on a sacrifce fly. The Mets went into the top of the ninth with a 4–2 lead. Armando Benitez came on in relief of John Franco, who had pitched the eighth inning and would be the winning pitcher if Benitez could shut the door on the Yankees. Benitez put the Yankees down and the Mets ended the Yankees' postseason winning streak. Mets fans hoped the third game would be the spark that would ignite their team.

The Yankees cooled the Mets newly found momentum early in Game Four. Once again a crowd of 55,777 saw the Yankees go to work early. Derek Jeter took the first pitch from Bobby Jones over the wall and circled the bases. It was also the first time in 157 World Series games that someone had homered on the first pitch. The Yankees had the lead and they would never lose it. The Bronx Bombers would add to it in the second and third innings. In the second inning Paul O'Neill hit a triple and came across on a Scott Brosius sac fly. In the third inning, Jeter tripled and scored on a ground ball by second baseman Luis Sojo. Then Mike Piazza cut the Yankees' lead to 3–2 with a two-run homer off Yankee starter Denny Neagle.

When Piazza came up in the fifth with two outs Neagle was pulled and David Cone came in. Piazza popped up to end the inning.

Pitching dominated the rest of the game and the Yankees' relievers Jeff Nelson, Mike Stanton, and closer Mariano Rivera didn't allow a Mets runner to reach second base. Mets' pitchers were also potent as Glendon Rusch, John Franco, and Armando Benitez did not allow the Yankees to score for the rest of the game. But, the Yankees took the game 3–2. Jeff Nelson was the winning pitcher and Bobby Jones took the loss.

The Yankees now had a commanding lead going into Game Five and stood one game away from their twenty-sixth World Championship.

The Mets put their hopes on the strong left arm of Al Leiter. The Yankees countered with Andy Pettitte. Pettitte lasted seven innings and was replaced by Mike Stanton in the bottom of the eighth with the score standing at two runs apiece.

Leiter continued to pitch into the ninth inning. He had thrown 121 pitches and had K'd seven Yankees on only two hits, but both had been costly solo home runs by Bernie Williams and Derek Jeter. Leiter struck out Tino Martinez and Paul O'Neill. He had thrown 129 pitches when up stepped Yankee catcher Jorge Posada. The Yankees backstop took Leiter deep in the count and walked after nine pitches. Leiter would face the right-handed hitter Scott Brosius.

Despite the hefty pitch count Valentine stayed with Leiter. The Mets bullpen aces Benitez and Franco had pitched the last two days and Valentine thought Leiter had enough in his tank to get the last out of the inning. Brosius singled to left, moving Posada to second base. Leiter had now thrown 141 pitches but he threw a fastball at the Yankees second baseman, Luis Sojo, who, with an awkward swing, slapped the ball between second base and short, into centerfield. Posada roared around the bases with the winning run. Payton fired the ball to Mike Piazza, but the ball's journey en route to the plate and the awaiting Piazza struck Posada on the hip and went rolling into the Met dugout. Posada and Brosius both came home to make the score 4–2. Bobby Valentine finally relieved Al Leiter, bringing in John Franco who ended the inning.

At midnight, with two out in the bottom of the ninth and the Yankees clinging to their 4–2 lead, Mariano Rivera fired a pitch to Mike Piazza. Piazza took the pitch deep with a runner on first. The sellout crowd roared and went to their feet but Bernie Williams caught up to it at the warning track in center field.

The Yankees had won the game, the Series, and their fourth World Series in five years.

For the Mets there was little to be ashamed of. They won the NL pennant and battled the Yankees to within a run in all but one of the games. Mets fans went to bed that night with the old lingering Brooklyn battle cry "Wait 'til Next Year."

THE METS 2001 SEASON

The Mets struggled during the 2001 season as they attempted to defend their 2000 NL Championship title. The Mets finished in third place behind the Braves, who claimed their 10th consecutive NL East flag.

Injuries hurt the Met offense during the 2001 season. Edgardo Alfonzo battled back problems and eventually ended up on the disabled list towards the end of the season. The second baseman hit .243 with 17 home runs, far from his 2000 season average of .324 and 25 home runs. Also spending time on the DL were outfielders Benny Agbayani and Jay Payton. Payton, who had been off to a fast start in the 2001 season, tore his hamstring in a game against the Colorado Rockies and missed two months of action.

These injuries opened up playing time for Japanese import Tsu-yoshi Shinjo. The slick-fielding Shinjo hit .268 during the season with 10 home runs. Though it was his first year in the big leagues, the Japanese outfielder played like a wily ten-year veteran.

The Mets pitching held firm in 2001, despite losing ace pitcher Mike Hampton to Colorado. Al Leiter, despite spending a month on the DL for a strained left elbow, managed to win 11 games with an ERA of 3.31. Kevin Appier and Steve Trachsel, whom the Mets picked up in the off-season, both picked up 11 wins apiece. Trachsel had a turnaround season after he was shipped back to the minors. The right-hander started the season with a 1–9 record, but finished with a 11–13 record. In the bullpen, Armando Benitez set a team record with 43 saves in 46 opportunities.

The Mets spent most of the season under .500. Finally on September 18th, after 141 regular season games, the Mets pulled themselves up to .500. They became the hottest team in the National League from late August to early October, winning 26 games against 9 losses, putting them back into the pennant race with the Braves and the Phillies.

When the season resumed, after nearly a week hiatus due to the attacks in New York and the Pentagon, the dream for another pennant ran out on the Mets as they lost 10–1 to the Pirates, elim-inating them from the race.

One bright spot in the disappointing season was Lenny Harris, who became the all-time pinch-hit champion with 151 pinch hits in his fourteen-year career.

However the Mets do though, fans will always follow and root for their team as they have since the days of Casey Stengel and Marv Throneberry, uttering the battle cry "Ya Gotta Believe!"

Opening day at Shea Stadium, April 1964.
Casey Stengel and Joan Payson.

Casey tunes up the orchestra with Guy Lombardo and the
Royal Canadians. Opening day, Shea Stadium, April 1964.

Banner Day 1965, Shea Stadium. The dream
would be realized in four years.

Heroes of Flatbush reunite at the Polo Grounds in 1962. *(Left to right)*:
Gil Hodges, Clem Labine, Don Newcombe, Charlie Neal, and Roger Craig.

Ron Hunt attempts to tag out Henry Aaron
during a game at Shea Stadium.

Tom Seaver.

Heroes of the 1969 season reunite at an Old-Timers Game at Shea Stadium. *(Left to right)*: Tommie Agee, Ron Swoboda, and Jerry Grote.

Jerry Grote tags out Pete Rose at Shea.

The miracle moment: The Mets celebrate the final out
in the final game of the 1969 World Series.

Mets manager Yogi Berra and Pirates manager
Bill Virdon shake before the game.

Yankee Manager Billy Martin confers with Mets Manager
Joe Torre at Shea Stadium.

Rusty Staub with his mother during Rusty Staub Day
at Shea Stadium.

Tug McGraw and Jerry Koosman at the 1987 Old-Timers
Game at Shea Stadium.

Darryl Strawberry swings away in a game at Shea Stadium.

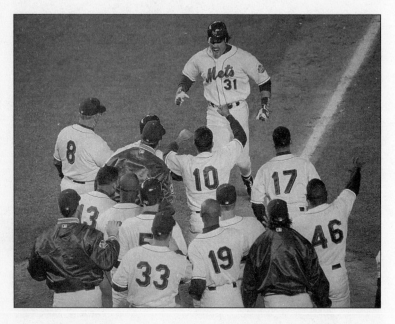

Mike Piazza is swarmed by teammates after a home run.

Notable Mets

CASEY STENGEL

If any man was worthy of being the Mets first manager it was the beloved Charles Dillon Stengel. The Kansas City native learned his baseball early on as an outfielder for the legendary coach John McGraw in the 1920s. Stengel patrolled major league outfields for two decades with the Brooklyn Dodgers, Philadelphia Phillies, New York Giants, and Boston Braves. Stengel ended his solid playing career with a lifetime .284 batting average and the former dentist decided to test the managerial waters.

Stengel managed five teams in both the major and minor leagues from the time of his retirement as a player in 1925 until being hired by the Yankees in 1949.

Stengel-managed major league teams never rose higher than fifth place in the eight-team leagues. He managed the Dodgers for three years in the mid-'30s and when he was fired in Brooklyn he signed with the Boston Braves and managed them from 1938 through 1943.

In those years Casey Stengel's reputation grew, Not for his managing or field generalship but for his wit and prankster behavior. In one game, Stengel took off his cap and a bird flew out of it, and he often donned raincoats to coax rain delays.

In 1949 the Yankees decided to give the fifty-nine-year-old Stengel one last shot as a big league manager and it paid off. Stengel had been managing Oakland in the Pacific Coast League and took Oakland to a PCL tittle in 1948—their first pennant in twenty-one years. That accomplishment would pale in comparison to his efforts with the Yankees.

During Stengel's reign the Yankees won ten pennants in twelve years and from 1949 through 1953 the Yankees won five consecutive World Series. In 1960, after the Yankees lost to the Pittsburgh Pirates, the seventy-year-old Stengel was let go by the Yankees.

In 1962 the fledgling Mets called on the irascible Stengel to manage the team and Stengel held that job from their first season until a hip injury sidelined him and later forced his retirement in 1965 at the still-young age of seventy-five.

Under Stengel the Mets enjoyed little success, winning only 175 games and losing 404 and never rising out of the National League basement. But Stengel entertained the press and Mets fans alike with his antics and insights, and made the early Mets teams lovable. Stengel's quotes have become part of New York baseball lore and following is a sampling of the wit and wisdom of Charles Dillon Stengel.

On bonus baby Ed Kranepool: "He may be only seventeen, but he runs like he's thirty."

"I'll never make the mistake of being seventy again."

"Most people my age are dead at the present time, and you could look it up."

"All right, everyone, line up alphabetically according to your height."

"The only thing worse than a Mets game is a Mets double-header."

"I was such a dangerous hitter I even got intentional walks in batting practice."

"The Mets have shown me more ways to lose than I even knew existed."

Casey Stengel was inducted into the Baseball Hall of Fame in 1966 and passed away in 1975 at the age of eighty-five.

MARV THRONEBERRY

No player epitomized the hapless Mets more than their first baseman Marvin Eugene Throneberry, whose initials spelled out M-E-T. The Tennessee native just seemed to have a knack at being at the wrong place at the wrong time and bringing baseball ineptness to a new art form.

Throneberry joined the Mets in a trade with the Baltimore Orioles that sent catcher Hobie Landrith to Baltimore a month into the 1962 season.

The twenty-nine-year-old Throneberry was no stranger to New York. He had been a Yankee for three years, mostly riding the bench. Some in the Yankee organization viewed him as a Mickey Mantle lookalike. Unfortunately, that's where the similarities ended. Throneberry also had stints with the A's and the Orioles before he became a Met.

It was as a Met that Throneberry (or "Marvelous Marv" as he was called by the press and the fans) blossomed. The free-swinging, sloppy-fielding, and tortoise-slow Throneberry won Mets fans over with his hustle which always seemed to come just short of the desired results.

A contract dispute in 1963 ended Throneberry's career with the Mets, and it also ended his major league career. Not many teams were in line to sign the lifetime .237 hitter to a contract.

Throneberry resurfaced twenty years after his playing career ended as a comic figure in beer commercials. Marv Throneberry died on June 23, 1994. He was sixty-one years old.

AL JACKSON

The little left-hander that the Mets acquired from the Pirates in the expansion draft proved to be the ace of the Mets pitching staff during those horrendous early years and might arguably have been the best Mets pitcher before the arrival of Tom Seaver.

Jackson pitched four shut-outs during the 1962 season and pitched an entire 15 innings for a loss to the Phillies 3–1. The twenty-six-year-old Jackson threw 215 pitches in that loss—an unheard-of feat by today's standards.

The Texan's 13–17 record in 1963 was quite an accomplishment considering the ineptitude that surrounded him as the Mets lost 111 games. His 43 wins with the Mets stood as a team record untill the arrival of Tom Seaver.

At the end of the 1965 season, the twenty-nine-year-old Jackson was traded to the St. Louis Cardinals for third baseman Ken Boyer. Al Jackson pitched for the Cards in the 1966 and 1967 seasons, finishing with a 22–21 mark.

Jackson rejoined the Mets for the 1968 season and checked out with a 3–7 record. He finished his career with the Reds in 1969. Al Jackson's career stats stood at 67 wins and 99 losses and a very respectable ERA of 3.98.

ED KRANEPOOL

This Bronx native and bonus baby signed with the Mets for $85,000 after his graduation from James Monroe High School. While at Monroe, Kranepool drew comparisons with another slugging Bronx first baseman who attended Monroe by the name of Hank Greenberg.

Kranepool came to the Mets in 1962 and would stay through

the 1979 season. His eighteen years of service were the longest in Mets history.

Though he had stints in the outfield, the tall, husky Kranepool was a fixture at first base for the better part of two decades. In his early years with the hapless Mets, Kranepool struggled at the plate and on the field. These struggles led one New York daily newspaper to print a headline when Kranepool was nineteen, IS KRANEPOOL OVER THE HILL?

He soon found his niche and started hitting major league pitching. Taking over first base after Marv Throneberry departed, the lumbering Kranepool showed himself to be a reliable fielder and adequate hitter.

Kranepool was also a deadly pinch hitter and in 1974 led the National League with 17 pinch hits and a major league leading average in his pinch-hit role of .486. He hit .396 as a pinch hitter from 1974–1978.

Ed Kranepool retired after the end of the 1979 season. He would leave baseball as the all-time Met leader in eight offensive categories. Kranepool would finish his career with a .261 batting average and 118 home runs.

After baseball, Kranepool would try his hand as a stockbroker and a restauranteur.

TOM SEAVER

The greatest pitcher in the history of the New York Mets was born in Fresno, California, in 1944. Seaver was an outstanding baseball prospect at USC. He originally signed with the Braves, but the signing was voided by Baseball Commissioner William Eckert, (the rule stated that a college ballplayer was off limits to big league baseball after the college season began) which made Seaver eligible to any team that matched the Braves offer. The

Indians, Phillies, and Mets were willing but the Mets were picked in the random drawing held in the commissioner's office. Tom Seaver signed with the Mets in 1966 and the rest is history.

Seaver's rise in the Mets organization was meteoric. The following year he was in Mets pinstripes and wooing the fans and media across the nation.

In 1967, Seaver's rookie year, the charismatic twenty-two-year old captured 16 wins, made the All-Star team, and won Rookie of the Year honors, but better things would follow.

Tom Seaver fueled the Mets in their 1969 World Championship when he won 25 games against 7 losses with an ERA of 2.21. In addition he flirted with a perfect game on July 9, 1969, only to see Jimmy Qualls destroy that effort with a single with one out in the 9th. Seaver captured the first of three Cy Young Awards in 1969 and would be one of the NL's most dominant pitchers for more than a decade.

In a game in 1970 Seaver struck out 19 Padres, including 10 in a row. In 1971 (which Tom Seaver would claim was his best season) he recorded 20 wins, led the National League in strikeouts with two hundred and eighty-nine and had an ERA of 1.76.

"Tom Terrific" as he was affectionately called by many of the Shea faithful, picked up his second Cy Young Award as the Mets prevailed in the "Ya Gotta Believe" year of 1973 where a weak hitting, but hustling, Mets team went to the World Series. In 1973 Seaver became the first non-20-game-winner to take the Cy Young Award. He totaled 19 wins and once again led the National League in strikeouts with 251, and had an ERA of 2.08.

The anemic Mets offense plagued Tom Seaver in Game One of the 1973 NLCS. Seaver drove in the Mets only run with a base hit but the run didn't stand as the Reds reached Seaver for solo home runs in the eighth and ninth innings by Pete Rose and Johnny Bench. Seaver was tagged with the loss even though he struck out 13 Reds and walked none. Seaver came back in Game Five to clinch the series for the Mets 7–2 and gave up only one earned run.

Seaver pitched well in the World Series that year against the Oakland A's, striking out 12 in eight innings of Game Three but he got a no-decision as the Mets were bested by the A's 3–2. He pitched well in Game Six giving up only two runs in his seven innings of work, but still took the loss as the Mets went down 3–1.

In 1974 a sore hip hindered Seaver as the right-hander finished with an 11–11 mark and an ERA of 3.20—very unSeaver-like numbers. But, "Tom Terrific" bounced back in 1975.

Seaver took the Cy Young Award for the third time in 1975 finishing with a 22–9 record and leading the league in wins, winning percentage, and strikeouts.

Despite his prowess on the mound there were problems ahead for Seaver with Mets General Manager M. Donald Grant. Seaver and Grant disagreed over how the Mets were being run and over Seaver's salary. The disputes grew bitter and on June 15, 1977, Seaver was dealt to the Cincinnati Reds for four players. Met fans mourned Seaver and cursed Grant.

Tom Seaver thrived in Cincinnati. The Big Red Machine was still largely intact with Pete Rose, Johnny Bench, Joe Morgan, and George Foster. Seaver finished the 1977 season with a combined 21–6 record and led the National League with seven shutouts.

On June 16, 1978, almost a year to the day that Seaver was traded to the Reds, the Gods of Baseball smiled down on "Tom Terrific" as he pitched a no-hitter against the St. Louis Cardinals in a 4–0 Reds win.

Seaver continued to pitch for the Reds through the 1982 season. He enjoyed his best season during that span in the strike-shortened season of 1981. Seaver went 14–2 and led the majors in wins and lost a controversial Cy Young vote to the Dodgers' Fernando Valenzuela.

The thirty-eight-year-old Seaver found himself traded back to New York for the 1983 season for three players. Seaver won nine games for another weak-hitting Mets team but still posted a respectable ERA of 3.55.

One of the biggest foul-ups in the history of the Mets occurred after 1983 when Tom Seaver was left unprotected in the free agent compensation pool by the Mets and plucked from New York by the Chicago White Sox.

Seaver prospered in Chicago, winning thirty-one games during the 1984 and 1985 seasons. 1985 held a few landmarks for Seaver. On August 4, at Yankee Stadium, he pitched his 300th win and completed all nine innings to beat the Yankees 4–1 on six hits. On October 4, Tom Seaver moved past Walter Johnson to put himself in third place on the all-time strikeout list.

Seaver was traded to the Red Sox in 1986 and finished his injury-ridden season with a 5–7 mark. An ankle injury kept the forty-one-year-old Seaver out of the 1986 Series. That year was Seaver's last season as he shortly announced his retirement. Since his playing days have ended he entered the broadcasting booth, handling Mets telecasts along with the legendary Ralph Kiner and Gary Thorne.

Tom Seaver was inducted into the Baseball Hall of Fame in 1992 with career marks of 311 wins, a .603 winning percentage, and 3,640 strikeouts.

RON HUNT

This gutsy second baseman was the Mets first All-Star in 1964 and fittingly played at Shea Stadium with the World's Fair going on across Roosevelt Avenue in Flushing Meadow Park, adjacent to the newly opened Shea.

The Missouri native came up to the Mets in 1963, hit .272 and had 10 home runs. He played second base with the expertise of a ten-year veteran.

The following season Hunt made his first of two All-Star appearances as he hit .303 on a Mets team that would end up losing 112 games. But, Hunt gave Mets fans much to cheer about with his all-out aggressive play and sparkling fielding.

Hunt was adept at getting on base via the base hit, walk, or yes, getting plunked by pitches. In that category Hunt was World Class.

In his twelve-year career with the Mets, Dodgers, Giants, Expos, and Cardinals, Hunt was hit by a pitch 243 times, 50 pitches in the 1971 season, and was once tagged by three in one game. Hunt commented, "Some people give their body to science. I give my body to baseball."

He made his second All-Star team in 1966, but at season's end was traded to the Dodgers for Tommy Davis. The twenty-five-year-old second baseman was heartbroken but would go on to have a distinguished major league career.

Hunt finished his career at the end of the 1974 season with a lifetime .273 batting average. Since baseball Ron Hunt has become a rancher outside of his native St. Louis and also runs a baseball camp for boys 15–18 years of age.

CLEON JONES

The 1969 Championship season was one of highs and lows for this Mets outfielder. He finished third in the National League batting race with a .340 average on a team that was not known for its offensive pop. The low mark of the 1969 season for Cleon Jones was on July 30, in a doubleheader against the Astros. On that day manager Gil Hodges took a long walk from the dugout to left field and replaced Jones for not hustling after an Astro base hit. Hodges' actions sparked a message to the World Series-bound Mets that nothing less than total effort would be tolerated.

Cleon Jones rebounded and the twenty-six-year-old Alabama native enjoyed his finest season in the big leagues. Jones also led the Mets with ten game-winning RBIs in the 1969 season. He would also be a catalyst in the Mets 1973 pennant drive with his timely hitting and defensive play.

It was a stellar defensive play and throw by Jones that propelled the Mets into first place late in the 1973 season. With Rich Zisk of the Pirates on first base and the score tied 3–3 in the ninth inning, Dave Augustine sent a pitch deep for an apparent home run. The ball hit the top of the wall. Jones caught the ball off the wall and relayed his throw to Wayne Garrett at third base who nailed Zisk at home. The Mets went on to win in the thirteenth inning and took first place.

Cleon Jones was released by the Mets in 1975. He would sit out the 1975 season but finish his career with the White Sox in 1976.

Jones left baseball with a .281 batting average and 94 lifetime home runs during his 12-year career.

JERRY KOOSMAN

If Tom Seaver was the top right-hander in the franchise's history than "Kooz" has to be the top left-hander. This pitching duo gave the Mets their all-time right–left combo and baffled National League batting lineups for many years.

Koosman's first full season with the Mets was 1968 and although the Mets struggled and finished in ninth place with a 73–89 record, this Minnesota native captured the National League's Rookie Pitcher of the Year Award with 19 wins and an ERA of 2.08. A record that still stands for a Mets rookie.

In the World Championship year and Koosman's sophomore season, the left-hander won 17 games against 9 losses and claimed 2 wins against the Orioles in the World Series.

With the Mets, he was a consistent top-level major league pitcher whose main strength was his control. Koosman battled arm problems during the 1971 season and in the Mets pennant-winning season of 1973 won 14 games and lost 15, despite having a fine ERA of 2.84.

Jerry Koosman had his finest season in 1976 when he won 21 games against 10 losses. After the Mets traded Tom Seaver near the midway point of the 1977 season the Mets went south in the standings finishing last in the NL East. Koosman lost 20 games that year with only 8 wins.

In December 1978, Koosman was dealt to the Minnesota Twins for reliever Jesse Orosco. Koosman rebounded, pitching in his native state and finishing the 1979 season with a 20–13 mark.

Jerry Koosman would later pitch for the White Sox and the Phillies. He retired from baseball in 1985 with a 222–209 record and a career ERA of 3.36.

GIL HODGES

"Why isn't this man in the Hall of Fame?" New York baseball fans ask when they think of the legendary Brooklyn Dodgers first baseman and Mets manager. This beloved Hoosier who was one of Brooklyn's favorite adopted sons hit .273 with 370 home runs during a playing career that spanned 3 decades.

Gilbert Ray Hodges of Princeton, Indiana, came up to the Brooklyn Dodgers at nineteen at the tail-end of the 1943 season. Hodges's Big League debut was less than inspiring. He played third base, struck out twice, and walked. In a matter of weeks Hodges exchanged his Dodger uniform for the uniform of the U.S. Marine Corps.

Hodges fought on Okinawa and earned a Bronze Star in the spring of 1945. In 1947, he rejoined the Dodgers as a catching prospect, but was told by manager Leo Durocher to pick up a first baseman's glove and to begin working at first base. There was a future Hall of Fame catcher by the name of Roy Campanella the Dodgers had their eyes on for the backstop slot. The move would benefit both Campanella and Hodges.

For the next ten years Gil Hodges was the quiet leader on the Dodgers. A man of few words, gentlemanly demeanor, and Herculean strength, Hodges was arguably the most respected and beloved of all the players on the team.

A slump in the 1952 World Series against the hated Yankees motivated Brooklyn priests and parishioners to offer prayers for Gil Hodges who was struggling through an 0–21 slump. However, there weren't many slumps in the illustrious career of Gil Hodges.

On August 31, 1950, the Dodgers' first baseman slugged four home runs in one game against the Boston Braves. In 1951 the twenty-seven-year-old slugged 40 home runs for the Flatbush faithful, two shy of Ralph Kiner's league-leading mark of 42 that the future Mets broadcaster hit for the Pittsburgh Pirates. Hodges' best season was 1954 when he hit .304, with 42 home runs, and 130 RBIs.

Hodges was a model of consistency in Flatbush, knocking in 100 runs or more for seven consecutive seasons between 1949–1955. He was also a pull hitter who took advantage of the short left-field fence at Ebbets Field.

When the unthinkable happened at the end of the 1957 season and the Dodgers moved to Los Angeles, Hodges continued to make his home in Brooklyn. And although he continued to play well in Los Angeles, the best days of his career had been left in Brooklyn.

The Mets took Hodges in the expansion draft of 1962. He hit the first regular season game homer in the history of the Mets, but injuries dogged him throughout the season. He finished the year batting .252 with 9 home runs. In 1963 Hodges was dealt to the Washington Seantors for outfielder Jimmy Piersall.

For Hodges, the move to Washington was more than a trade— it was a career change. He never played a game at first base for the struggling Washington franchise that was the doormat of the American League. Hodges managed the Senators and in his five-year reign turned this joke of a team into a respectable, competitive group of overachievers. Mets management took notice and in 1968 Gil Hodges once again put on a Mets uniform.

Change was immediately apparent during the 1968 season. Under Hodges's strong, quiet confidence the Mets rose out of the basement and for only the second time in the team's seven-year history, it didn't finish in last place. Many New York baseball observers believed a large part of the improvement was due to the quiet marine and Brooklyn Dodgers hero.

Gil Hodges's crowning achievement in baseball was his guidance of the Mets to the 1969 World Championship. Many of his on-field moves bordered on genius as he platooned his weak-hitting 1969 team in five positions and, under his tutelage, his young pitching staff continued to mature and develop. In 1969 John Lindsay was re-elected mayor of New York City but Gil Hodges could easily have beaten him.

Hodges died of a heart attack during spring training on April 2, 1972, a few days short of his 48th birthday. The baseball world mourned the strong but gentle Hoosier. His career record as manager of the Mets was 339–309 for a winning percentage of .523, but, Gil Hodges was always a winner.

TOMMIE AGEE

The Mets obtained Tommie Lee Agee from the Chicago White Sox prior to the 1968 season for Tommy Davis. It was hoped that the Alabama native would supply the Mets lineup with the speed and power it was sorely lacking.

Agee struggled in his first year in New York hitting only .217 with 5 home runs. The pressure was on Agee to have a big year in 1969 and he did.

In that championship season, Agee led the Mets in home runs with 26. Batting from the leadoff slot, Agee also led the pitching-dominated Mets team in RBIs with 76 and helped make the Mets championship run possible.

In the pivotal Game Three of the 1969 World Series, Agee nearly singlehandedly beat the Baltimore Orioles. Agee led off with a home run off of Hall of Fame pitcher Jim Palmer. Agee later saved the game for the Mets with two astounding plays in center field: a circus catch in the fourth inning off of Orioles catcher Elrod Hendricks, and his sliding catch to take an extra-base hit away from Orioles outfielder Paul Blair in the seventh inning with two outs and the bases loaded. Those two defensive gems saved five runs, gave the Mets a 5–0 victory over Baltimore, and made Tommie Agee a World Series hero for the ages.

He continued to wear Mets pinstripes through the 1972 season and would later play with the Astros and the Cards. He retired in 1973.

Tommie Agee died of a heart attack in January 2001. He was fifty-eight years old. Mets teammates Tug McGraw, Ed Charles, Donn Clendenon, Ed Kranepool, Art Shamsky, and Bud Harreslon served as pallbearers.

"In that miraculous year of 1969, he was very special to us," Ed Charles reminisced at Agee's funeral.

In his twelve-year career, Tommie Agee hit .255 with 130 home runs but will always be remembered for his heroics in the third game of the 1969 World Series.

BUD HARRELSON

The slightly built Californian was the anchor of the Mets infield from his rookie season in 1965 through the 1977 season. Harrelson is second on the Mets all-time list for games played and at bats.

Harrelson is considered one of the best shortstops in franchise history. He was the total package. His excellent fielding kept him in the lineup and although he rarely hit higher than .250 as a Met he was adept at getting on base. Once on base, his speed made him a threat to steal or take the extra base on a base hit.

Harrelson's top year was 1970. He went fifty-four games without making an error at short and reached career highs in five offensive categories. The following year Harrelson swiped twenty-eight bases and took the Gold Glove for his defensive play.

Mets fans will always remember the image of the 200-pound Pete Rose and the feisty 150-pound Harrelson coming to blows over the collision at second base during the third game of the 1973 NLCS.

Bud Harrelson was released by the Mets following the 1977 season but was picked up by the Philadelphia Phillies. Harrelson would play for the Phillies during the 1978 and 1979 seasons and concluded his career in the American League with the Texas Rangers in 1980.

The Mets called on Bud Harrelson to coach after his playing days were over. Harrelson was a coach from 1982 until 1990 when he succeeded Davey Johnson as the Mets manager less than halfway through the season.

Under Harrelson the Mets finished second in the NL East in 1990 with a 71–49 record. In Harrelson's second season (1991) the Mets played with little enthusiasm, ending up in last place. Harrelson's mark as Mets manager for the 1991 season stood at 74–80 when he was replaced in the last week of the season by interim manager Mike Cubbage. His record as Mets manager finished at 145–129.

During his major league playing career—that spanned from 1965 through 1980—the slick-fielding Harrelson averaged .236 with 7 home runs.

JERRY GROTE

Lou Brock once called Grote the toughest catcher to steal on. Grote was a rock behind home plate for the Mets for a dozen years, but Grote didn't become of the NL's top defensive catchers overnight. Jerry Grote struggled for many years and the former Houston Colt .45 blamed many for his shortcomings behind the plate and with the bat. It was a remark by then-manager Wes Westrum that turned Grote's fortunes around.

The former New York Giants catcher remarked, "If Grote ever learns to control himself he might become the best catcher in the game." The Texan took his manager's words to heart and did indeed become one of the top catchers in the NL in the later part of the 1960s and the 1970s. Grote caught every inning of the 1969 NLCS and World Series and every inning of the 1973 NLCS and World Series.

Grote later went on to catch for the Los Angeles Dodgers in their pennant-winning years of 1977 and 1978, and in 1981 the thirty-eight-year-old Grote was lured out of retirement by the Kansas City Royals where he hit .304 in 22 games.

During his 16-year career Grote finished with a .252 average and 39 home runs.

TUG McGRAW

He was the "Ya Gotta Believe" boy—the fun-loving relief pitcher that fueled the Mets miracle pennant drive of the 1973. But, during the 1973 season McGraw did more than coin pennant-winning phrases. McGraw won 5 games but in his role as fireman for the 1973 Mets the left-hander saved 25 more.

Frank Edwin McGraw came up to the Mets during the 1965 season and would be a mainstay in the Met bullpen for nearly a decade. His best season was 1972 when McGraw went 11–4 with 27 saves and an ERA of 1.70.

In December, 1974, the popular Californian was part of a six-player deal that sent him to the City of Brotherly Love. The Mets acquired John Stearns who would pay dividends for the Mets in years to come but New York Mets fans had lost a favorite.

With the Phillies, McGraw was once again one of the top relievers in the NL. He would wear a Phillies uniform for ten years and in the Phillies World Series winning year of 1980 he was one of the top relievers for Philadelphia with 20 saves and 5 wins.

In the World Series that year, McGraw is remembered for striking out Kansas City outfielder Jose Cardinal, after walking the bases loaded in the ninth inning, to preserve a Phillies win in Game Five. In the sixth and final game of the 1980 Series, McGraw pitched out of jams in the eighth and ninth innings to insure the Phillies victory and get himself a save.

In his 20-year career McGraw won 96 games against 92 losses and had 180 saves.

JON MATLACK

Big things were expected of John Matlack when the Mets made him their number one selection in the June 1967 draft. The Mets weren't disappointed five years later when the West Chester, Pennsylvania, native was the NL's Rookie of the Year.

In his rookie year of 1972 Matlack went 15–10 with an ERA of 2.32—fourth best in the NL. In the pennant-winning year of 1973, Matlack's pitching was strong and consistent despite his 14–16 record. The left-hander posted 205 strikeouts and finished the season with a respectable 3.20 ERA.

During the season a Marty Perez line-drive fractured Matlack's skull, but Matlack was back in action in less than two weeks. During Game Two of the NLCS against the Reds, Matlack threw a two-hit nine-strikeout game. Matlack also started three games of the 1973 World Series against the Oakland A's. Matlack pitched brilliantly in Game One, losing a 2–1 decision as the Mets gave Oakland the game with unearned runs in the third inning. Matlack pitched another masterpiece in Game Four getting the win and giving up three hits in eight innings. Unfortunately, Matlack wasn't up to the task in Game Seven as the A's knocked him out of the game in the third inning, and he lost the game—and the Mets lost the series.

Matlack was hurt by the weak-hitting Mets teams of the mid-'70s. In 1974 his 2.41 ERA was third best in the NL, but he had a losing record of 13–15.

Matlack reached his peak as a pitcher the next two seasons, winning 33 games and losing 22. He was also the winning pitcher in the 1975 All-Star game as he struck out four American Leaguers in two innings. During the 1976 season Matlack pitched six shutouts, posted an ERA of 2.94, and threw 16 complete games.

Matlack slumped in 1977, finishing with a 7–15 record and an ERA of 4.21. He was dealt to the Texas Rangers at season's end in a four-team deal.

With the Rangers he rebounded in 1978 and was one of the top hurlers in the American League, winning 15 games and losing 13 and posting the second best ERA in the AL at 2.27.

Matlack missed most of the 1979 season with elbow problems and along with the shoulder problems that recurred during his career, these injuries would hasten the end of his career after the 1983 season.

Matlack's career numbers are 125 wins and 126 losses and a 3.18 ERA with 30 shutouts.

FELIX MILLAN

Nicknamed the "Cat," Felix Millan was a vital cog in the Mets pennant drive of 1973. The surehanded Millan came over from Atlanta in one of the best trades in Mets franchise history. The Puerto Rico–native came to the Mets from Atlanta with pitcher

George Stone, who finished 12–3 for the Mets in 1973, for pitchers Gary Gentry and Danny Frisella.

Millan broke in with Atlanta in 1968 and was a major contributor in the Braves first-place finish in the NL West in 1969. In 1970 Millan batted .310 and during his career was considered one of the toughest men in the NL to strike out. On July 6, 1970, Milan went 6–6. He was placed on the NL All-Star team for the 1969, 1970, and 1971 seasons. After a subpar performance in 1972, Millan was traded to the Mets.

Millan was a spark plug for the Mets from 1973 through 1977. He was a dependable second baseman and a good hitter. In one game in 1975, Millan had four straight singles but was taken out each time when Joe Torre grounded into four consecutive double plays to the Astros. Millan's career ended prematurely on August 12, 1977, when he suffered a broken collarbone in a brawl with Pirates catcher Ed Ott.

During Millan's twelve-year career he averaged .279 with 22 home runs.

RUSTY STAUB

One of the most popular of all Mets, Daniel Joseph Staub was signed by the Houston Colt .45s for $100,000 in 1961. At the age of nineteen Staub played 150 games for the Colt .45s in 1963. During that season Staub hit his first home run. Twenty-three years later, in 1985, Rusty Staub would hit his last home run, making Staub and Ty Cobb the only major leaguers to hit home runs as teenagers and after their fortieth birthdays.

During a career that spanned three decades, Staub was one of the most dangerous hitters in baseball. He played for four teams: the Astros, Expos, Mets (twice), and the Tigers. He is the only man to have played for four teams and collect five hundred or more hits for each of them.

During his prolific years with the Expos after he was traded to Montreal in January of 1969, Staub became a fan favorite by the French-Canadian fans who nicknamed him "Le Grand Orange" because of his red hair. He was the expansion Expos first star, hitting 30 home runs in the 1970 season and being named to the NL All-Star team.

Rusty Staub was traded to the Mets for outfielder Ken Singleton, utility player Mike Jorgensen, and infielder Tim Foli just prior to the beginning of the 1972 season.

Staub became a fan favorite in New York. He was well versed in gourmet cooking and history and led one observer to claim, "He leads the league in idiosyncrasies."

Injuries hampered Staub in his first two season with the Mets but he showed fans he could hit. In his injury-shortened 1972 season Staub hit .293 and in 1973 hit .279 with 15 home runs.

Rusty Staub had some of his greatest career moments and perhaps one of his most horrible as well. On October 8th in the NLCS against the Reds, Staub homered in the first and second inning of Game Three of the 1973 NLCS, sparking the Mets 9–2 win over Cincinnati. It was in the fourth game of that series that Rusty Staub smashed into the right-field wall taking an extra base hit away from the Reds' Dan Driessen.

Staub took cortisone shots and threw underhanded from the outfield: despite the bad shoulder Staub wasn't going to sit out the World Series.

On October 17 against the A's in the fourth game of the 1973 World Series, Rusty Staub went 4 for 4 with a home run in the Mets 6–1 win.

In 1975 the Mets sent Staub to the Detoit Tigers for pitcher Mickey Lolich. The All-Star pitcher never put up the numbers the Mets had envisioned for but Staub, who was used mainly in the DH role in the American League, thrived. In 1978 Staub knocked in 121 runs for the Tigers with 24 home runs.

The Tigers traded Staub back to Montreal midway through the

1979 season. He finished the season with the Expos and then was dealt by Montreal to the Texas Rangers. Staub returned to New York for the 1981 season and played through 1985 mainly as a very prolific pinch hitter. On June 26, 1983, in a game against the Phillies, Staub delivered his ninth consecutive pinch hit, tying Dave Philley for the all-time Major League record. Staub closed out the 1983 season with 25 RBIs as a pinch hitter, sharing the record with Joe Cronin and Jerry Lynch.

Staub saw at an early stage that his physical skills weren't as great as others. He was slow in the field and on the base paths but worked hard for his success as a ballplayer. Hall of Famer Duke Snider, who became a broadcaster for the Montreal Expos after his playing days were over, once said of Rusty Staub, "He is a pure hitter."

After he retired Staub became a well-known New York restaurateur. His restaurant "Rusty's" became a landmark on New York's Upper East Side. Staub is also an active philanthropist in New York.

Staub retired with 2,716 hits, a .279 batting average, and 292 home runs during his 23-year career.

JOHN STEARNS

In John Stearn's ten-year career with the Mets the Denver native made the NL All-Star team four times. As a catcher, Stearns was an all-around player: he was a line-drive hitter, a fine defensive catcher, and handled pitchers well. Despite all his abilities, however, Stearns was dogged with an assortment of injuries throughout his career.

Stearns had been the number-one pick for the Philadelphia Phillies in 1973, but, before that had been a grid-iron star at the University of Colorado, and had been drafted to play in the NFL by the Buffalo Bills.

As the Mets catcher Stearns brought an aggressive football

attitude to his play. He was also fleet and aggressive on the base paths, stealing 25 bases in 1978. He was disabled with elbow tendonitis in August 1982 and during the next two years played in just 12 games before he retired.

John Stearns hit .260 with 46 home runs during his major league career. During 2001 Stearns served the Mets as third-base coach.

CRAIG SWAN

Craig Swan was the Mets' top hurler in the late '70s, until a rotator cuff injury took away his fastball. His career spiraled downward in 1980, and a second arm injury in 1983 effectively ended his career.

Swan is best remembered by Mets fans as taking the NL ERA title in 1978 with a 2.43, despite only winning nine games and missing a month of the season with gastroenteritis.

Swan enjoyed his best season in the majors in 1979 racking up 14 wins against 13 losses with a 3.30 ERA. He was the work-horse of the Mets' pitching staff, completing 251 innings. At the end of the season, the Mets signed Swan to a five-year contract, the most lucrative in team history up to that point. Only months later, however, Swan would suffer his rotator cuff tear and his career and the Mets investment were never realized.

Swan finished his career with the California Angels in 1984, with 59 wins and 72 losses and an ERA of 3.75.

JOE TORRE

Before he collected his fourth World Series ring managing the New York Yankees, Joe Torre was learning his trade with the Mets as a rookie manager. Torre was playing third base for the Mets when he replaced manager Joe Frazier.

In his 18-year playing career, Torre was one of the most feared hitters in the NL and spanned three positions. Torre was recruited by the Milwaukee Braves as a catcher. Later, he would play third- and first base. Torre was also named to the NL All-Star team nine times, and he was NL MVP in 1971 hitting .363 with 24 home runs, and 137 RBIs.

As a Met Torre saw spot duty at third and first base. In 1975, he hit .247 with 6 home runs. In 1976, Torre's last full year as a player, he hit .306 with 6 home runs.

Torre was named as Joe Frazier's successor on May 31, 1977. Torre continued to play for another 18 days then he took himself off the active roster. Torre was the first player-manager in the NL in two decades.

Torre enjoyed little success as manager of the Mets. They never enjoyed a winning season, and their best finish was fourth in the strike-shortened split season of 1981. The Mets fired Torre at the end of the '81 season.

Torre later managed the Atlanta Braves from '82–84, then pulled a stint in the broadcast booth for the California Angels. He returned to manage the St. Louis Cardinals from 1990–1995.

Before his success with the Yankees Torre took the Braves to an NL East flag in 1982 but, until recently, his career in the dugout was marginal. Torre took the Yankee manager's job starting in 1996 and the rest is history.

BOBBY VALENTINE

Valentine first put on a Mets' uniform in the late '70s, coming over from San Diego in the Dave Kingman trade. Valentine was used as a utility infielder for the Mets but, by the end of the 1978 season at the age of twenty-eight, his career was over. A leg injury cut short what promised to be a bright, possibly All-Star career.

Valentine was the fifth player taken in the June 1968 draft. As a Connecticut high school grid-iron hero Valentine turned down many scholarship offers to sign with the Dodgers. He was the Pacific Coast League Player of the Year, batting .340. Valentine played on the Dodgers until 1972 when he was traded to the California Angels.

Valentine got off to a flying start with the Angels hitting .302, but on May 17, 1973, while playing centerfield, Valentine crashed into the outfield wall while chasing a ball hit by the Oakland A's Dick Green. Valentine suffered a serious spiral fracture that curtailed his promising career.

Bobby Valentine made his debut as manager with the Texas Rangers in 1986, after a stint as a Mets' coach from 1983–1985. He stayed in Texas for seven seasons. His teams were always in the thick of the pennant race, but the flag always eluded him. He was fired after the 1992 season.

Valentine continued to manage, taking a job in Japan. He was the first foreigner to manage a Japanese team during the 1995 season but at season's end was fired by the Chiba Lotte Marines.

The Mets soon hired Valentine to manage Norfolk, their top minor league team, and in 1996 they brought Valentine back to manage the Mets.

The Mets enjoyed their first winning season since 1990 under Valentine. In 1999 they made the playoffs, and went to the World Series in 2000.

Despite turning the Mets' fortunes, Valentine's tenure as the Mets manager has often been marked by turmoil and sometimes team disharmony.

WALLY BACKMAN

As a second baseman Wally Backman was a table-setter with his speed and ability to get on base. Backman was a vital cog in the Mets' Championship team of 1986.

The hustling, switch-hitting Backman hit .320 in 1986 and scored 67 runs with only 387 at bats. During the 1986 season, Backman platooned with right-handed hitter Tim Teufel.

Backman was the Mets first pick in the June 1977 draft. Though he proved early on that he was an offensive threat, his erratic fielding kept him down on the farm until 1984 when his former Tidewater manager, Davey Johnson, decided to bring him up to the big leagues. The promotion paid off with 68 runs and 32 stolen bases in his first season. In 1995 Backman lead NL second basemen in fielding.

The Mets traded Backman to the Minnesota Twins in 1988 where he hit only .231 was often sidelined with shoulder problems.

Backman came back to the NL with the Pittsburgh Pirates. They put the former Met on third base. He hit .292 in 104 games for the NL East champion Pirates. Backman's stellar moment with the Pirates, and maybe in his career, came on April 27, 1990, when he went 6 for 6 against the Padres, becoming the first National Leaguer in 15 years to accomplish that feat.

Backman spent the 1991 and 1992 seasons with the Phillies in a utility role. He finished his career in 1993 with the Seattle Mariners.

Wally Backman averaged .275 with 10 home runs in 1,102 games in the major leagues.

GARY CARTER

Gary Carter was inducted into the Mets Hall of Fame during the 2001 season. Mets fans still wonder when the eleven-time All-Star catcher will be admitted to Cooperstown.

Carter came to the Mets in 1985 through a multiplayer deal that sent infielder/outfielder Hubie Brooks, catcher Mike Fitzgerald, outfielder Herm Winningham, and pitcher Floyd Youmans to Montreal.

Carter first came up in 1975 to the Expos. He finished second in NL Rookie of the Year voting, hitting .270 with 17 home runs. The twenty-one-year-old Carter played outfield and third base, but thanks to former Dodgers catcher Norm Sherry, Carter was transformed into a catcher. During 1976 Carter missed the first 60 games of the season with an injury.

In the late '70s and early '80s Carter was known for his clutch hitting and skill at handling pitchers. With the decline of Johnny Bench and his retirement in 1983, Carter was the most dominant catcher in the NL.

Carter was a stabilizing force with the Mets in the mid-'80s. He was named an All-Star from 1985–1988. In his first game as a Met on Opening Day against the Cardinals, Carter won the game with a home run in extra innings. Carter hit five home runs in a two-game span that September.

In the Mets' Championship season of 1986, the southern California native contributed his share to the heroics hitting .255, with 24 home runs, and 105 RBIs. But, it was in the World Series that Gary Carter made his presence known.

In Game Four at Fenway Park, Carter helped the Mets even the series at two games apiece by hitting two home runs. And during the classic Game Six on October 25, 1986, Carter once again came through for the Mets. With two outs in the bottom of the tenth, Carter sliced a Calvin Schiraldi pitch to left field for a single and kept the Mets alive in the game. They would go on to win that game 6–5 and the Series in Game Seven.

Gary Carter's career started to decline after that championship year. He hit .235 with 20 home runs in 1987. In 1988 Carter hit .242 with 11 home runs, and in 1989 he injured his knee and missed most of the season, hitting under .200. The Mets released the thirty-five-year-old Carter at the end of 1989.

Carter would go on to play with the San Francisco Giants in 1990, the Los Angeles Dodgers in 1991, and finished his career with Montreal in 1992.

RON DARLING

The Hawaiian–born, Yale University–educated pitcher was the Texas Rangers' first pick in 1981. He was dealt to the Mets for outfielder Lee Mazzilli in 1982.

Darling appeared in ten games for the Mets in 1983, and finished with a 1–3 record. In 1984, his full rookie season, Darling finished with a 12–9 record, but he acquired a reputation for being a hard luck pitcher with more than his share of no-decisions.

Overshadowed by the phenomenal Dwight Gooden, Darling was nonetheless named to the 1985 NL All-Star team with a 16–6 record and an ERA of 2.90.

In 1986, Darling contributed 15 wins and along with Dwight Gooden, Bobby Ojeda, and Sid Fernandez was part of one of the most dominant pitching staffs in all the big leagues. In the 1986 World Series, Darling lost Game One 1–0 on a three-hitter but came back to win Game Four.

Darling continued to pitch well for the next four-and-a-half seasons with the Mets, posting a 48–35 record. He was dealt to the Montreal Expos for reliever Tim Burke in July 1991. The Expos then sent Darling to the Oakland A's for a couple of minor league hurlers.

Ron Darling finished his career in Oakland in 1995. His top year in the AL was in 1992, when he finished with 15 wins and 10 losses.

Ron Darling pitched in over 2,300 innings during his 13-year career and had an overall record of 136–116 with a 3.87 ERA.

HOWARD JOHNSON

This former pitcher came to the Mets in a December 1984 trade for pitcher Walt Terrell. The switch-hitting Johnson was platooned with Ray Knight at third base, and although lacking range there, also played shortstop. When Knight left the Mets after 1986, "Hojo" was handed the third base job and soon blossomed into a star in the NL.

In 1997 Johnson hit 36 home runs, establishing a record for switch hitters in the NL (a record that he would break two years later). Also that season, Johnson and Strawberry became the first teammates in Major League Baseball history to hit 30 or more home runs and steal 30 or more bases.

From the late '80s to the early '90s, Johnson was one of the most feared hitters in the NL. He was named to the NL All-Star team in 1989 and 1991. In 1989, his career year with the Mets, he batted .287 and had 36 home runs, 104 runs scored, and 101 runs batted in. Johnson also stole 41 bases that year.

In 1991 Johnson became the second man, along with Bobby Bonds, to be a 30–30 man more than twice. Johnson swatted thirty-eight home runs, stole 30 bases and knocked in 117 runs.

Despite his hitting prowess, fielding was always a lost art for Johnson, no matter where the Mets put him. In 1991 Johnson made 31 errors.

The following year, 1992, saw the decline of Johnson's career. A hairline fracture of the wrist limited his playing time. He suited up in only 100 games. In 1993 a broken finger hampered him and he hit only .238 with 7 home runs in just 72 games.

The Mets didn't re-sign Johnson in 1994 and he signed with Colorado. Johnson hit only .211 that year with 10 home runs in just 93 games.

The following year Howard Johnson was sent to the Chicago Cubs. Johnson hit only seven home runs and was out of baseball by season's end.

Johnson has since served the Mets as a scout and is currently the batting coach for the Brooklyn Cyclones, the Mets single-A minor league team.

Johnson's career stats are a .249 batting average and 228 home runs.

RAY KNIGHT

A man of many achievements during the 1986 season, Knight was voted NL Comeback Player of the Year as he raised his batting average by 80 points and took the World Series MVP Award for his inspirational play in the Fall Classic.

Ray Knight broke in with the Reds first coming up in 1974. He stayed with Cincinnati in the '70s, and he eventually replaced the legendary Pete Rose at third base.

Knight was traded to Houston where he often played first base. After three years where he was traded to the Mets in 1984 for three minor leaguers.

Knight hit .280 his first season with the Mets. After a poor season in 1985 where he hit only .218, Mets batting coach Bill Robinson changed the third baseman's stance. It paid off, and Knight had one of his best seasons at the plate.

Knight, the 1986 World Series MVP, scored the winning run in the memorable sixth game against Boston, and his home run in Game Seven was a decisive blow.

Knight signed as a free agent with the Baltimore Orioles in 1987 and he hit .256 with 14 home runs. The following season Knight signed with the Tigers and hit .217 and played first, third, and was sometimes a DH. He was out of the game by 1989 but returned to manage the Cincinnati Reds in 1996 until halfway into the 1997 season when he was replaced by Jack McKeon. Knight's managerial record with the Reds was 124–139.

During his 13-year playing career, Ray Knight hit .271 with 84 home runs.

SID FERNANDEZ

Despite pitching two no-hitters in the minors this hefty Hawaiian was let go by the Dodgers in 1983. The Mets picked him up in a trade for infielder Bob Bailor and pitcher Carol Diaz.

Fernandez quickly showed the Mets his potential finishing 6–6 with a 3.50 ERA. The following season Fernandez baffled NL hitters with 180 strikeouts in 170 innings. He finished the year with a 9–9 record and a 2.80 ERA. It was often said his herky-jerky motion threw off batters because it appeared as if the ball was coming out of his uniform.

Fernandez played an important role in the Mets' Championship season of 1986 going 16–6. During the rest of the 1980s Fernandez was an effective pitcher, but, due to weight problems that caused knee injuries, and a loss of stamina, Fernandez never reached his potential. Fernandez was not re-signed by the Mets after the 1993 season. He signed with the Orioles but injuries plagued him in 1994, and he was released by Baltimore in 1995.

Fernandez pitched for the Phillies and Astros after leaving Baltimore. He went 6–1 for the Phillies in 1995 but arm and elbow injuries continued to hamper him and Fernandez was out of baseball by the end of the 1997 season.

During a career that spanned 12 years, Sid Fernandez went 114–96 with a 3.36 ERA.

DWIGHT GOODEN

Great things were expected of Dwight Gooden and the Mets made the Tampa native their number-one pick in the 1982 draft. He showed incredible form in 1983 with Lynchburg in the class-A Carolina League. During that season the eighteen-year-old Gooden struck out 300 batters in only 191 innings, and led the league in wins, ERA, and strikeouts.

The teenaged Gooden made it up to New York for Opening Day the following year at the insistence of the Mets new manager, Davey Johnson. Although Mets GM Frank Cahsen felt it would be prudent to keep the youngster on the Mets Triple-A minor league team at Tidewater for one more season, Johnson won out.

Gooden made his debut in the Houston Astrodome on April 7, 1984. He picked up his first win in the bigs that day and his initial outing was only a sampling of things to come.

Dwight Gooden won the 1984 NL Rookie of the Year Award. He struck out 276 hitters in only 218 innings, setting a major league strikeout record for rookies. Because of his strikeout prowess the teenaged Gooden earned the nickname "Doctor K" by Mets fans. He finished with a 17–9 record with a 2.60 ERA and he was also named to the NL All-Star team, the youngest All-Star ever.

The following year was a monster one for the young man from Florida. Gooden lead the league in wins with 24 against only 4 losses. He also led the league with a 1.53 ERA, strikeouts with 268, and complete games with 16. Gooden was an easy winner for the Cy Young Award. Few knew it at the time but young Dwight Gooden had reached his peak at twenty.

In the Championship year of 1986 Gooden had a strong season going 17–6, striking out 200 hitters in 250 innings, and had a fine ERA of 2.84. He pitched well in the NLCS against Houston, but was pinned with two losses against the Red Sox in the World Series. Many observers felt the previous year's Cy Young winner wasn't as overpowering as he had been in 1985. There were reasons for Gooden's fall from grace that became apparent the following season.

In early 1987 the twenty-one-year-old Gooden and his nephew Gary Sheffield, who would go on to have a fine major league career himself, were involved in an altercation with the Tampa police. Then, just before the start of the baseball season, Dwight Gooden checked himself into a drug rehabilitation program.

Gooden missed the first two months of the 1987 season but still finished with a 15–7 record. The Mets narrowly lost the division to the St. Louis Cardinals, and many put the onus for the Mets failure to repeat as NL East Champs on Gooden because of his two-month absence.

Gooden rebounded in 1988 with an 18–9 record and the Mets won the Eastern Division. The following year at the mid-point in the season, Gooden went down with a sore shoulder, and was lost for most of the year.

From 1987 until his release in 1994, Dwight Gooden was a pitcher with a number of good seasons but alcohol and drug abuse continued to disrupt his promising career. He was punished each time for his off-field offenses. Baseball Commissioner Bud Selig stepped into the Gooden controversy in September 1994 when he banned Gooden for the rest of the season and all of 1995.

Gooden admitted that he contemplated suicide but, in January of 1996, Yankee owner George Steinbrenner believed the former Mets whiz-kid had defeated his demons and signed Gooden to the Yankees. Gooden delivered. He compiled an 11–7 record and on May 14, against the Seattle Mariners, matched his early form by pitching a no-hitter. It appeared Gooden's stock was on the rise again.

A misdiagnosed hernia shelved Gooden for much of 1997 and when he was healthy his pitching was at best lackluster. The Yankees didn't offer Gooden a new contract, and Dwight Gooden signed with Cleveland for the 1998 season. His career with Cleveland was disappointing.

Gooden signed with the Astros for the 2000 season but was traded to his hometown team, the Tampa Bay Devil Rays. The Devil Rays released Gooden but he took one last gasp at the bigs and signed a minor league contract with the Yankees. Gooden came back up to the bigs with the Yankees and performed well, compiling a 3.36 ERA in 18 games.

Spring training 2001 saw Gooden opting for a pitching spot with the Yankees but a 7.90 ERA dimmed his hopes. He turned down reassignment, and retired from baseball that spring.

Mets fans will always think of Dwight Gooden as that phenomenal teenager with the blazing fastball and wicked curve who per- haps would have been the Mets greatest pitcher, eclipsing even Tom Seaver. But the party life, alcohol, and cocaine took away the dream from Gooden, and New York fans. We all wonder what might have been.

During his career Gooden rang up 194 wins against 112 losses.

MOOKIE WILSON

William Hayward Wilson was one of the most beloved Mets in team history. Met fans would serenade the outfielder and longtime leadoff man with cries of *Moooooo-kie* but, Mookie Wilson is best known in baseball lore for the ground ball hit that scooted under the legs of Bill Buckner in the sixth game of the 1986 World Series.

Wilson came up to the Mets in 1980 and it was quickly appar- ent that the Mets had a prize. He hit .276 for three consecutive seasons (1983–1985) and between .271 to .299 from 1981 through 1989. Wilson was also a terror on the bases, stealing 58 in 1983 and 54 in 1984.

Mookie's speed in the outfield helped make up for a weak arm. He was a good defensive outfielder and led NL outfielders with six double plays in 1984. In the latter part of the 1980s Mookie pla- tooned with Lenny Dykstra and he was traded to Toronto in the second half of the 1989 season for pitcher Jeff Musselman.

Wilson continued to play for the Blue Jays through 1991. He continues to serve the Mets as the team's first base coach.

In his distinguished career that spanned a dozen seasons Mookie Wilson hit .277 with 62 home runs. His stepson, Preston Wilson, is a star outfielder for of the Florida Marlins.

KEITH HERNANDEZ

Mets fans felt their team was on the right track when Keith Hernandez came to the Mets in one of the finest deals in team history. The Mets acquired the All-Star first baseman in 1983 for pitchers Neil Allen and Rick Ownbey in a mid-season trade with the Cardinals. As a Cardinal, Hernandez led the NL in hitting with a .344 average, and split the National League's MVP Award with the Pittsburgh Pirates' Willie Stargell. Hernandez had a reputation for being a carefree and easygoing player despite being a consistent hitter and a Gold Glove first baseman.

With the Mets, Hernandez took on a new intensity and was a solid clutch hitter batting out of the number three slot. He finished the 1983 season hitting .306 for the Mets, and took his sixth consecutive Gold Glove Award. Hernandez would collect eleven consecutive Gold Gloves from 1978–1988. At first base Hernandez was an aggressive fielder with great range and impeccable field judgment.

Hernandez's potent bat and solid glove made the Mets one of the top teams in baseball through the mid- to late-'80s. During those years Hernandez was named to the NL All-Star team three times and from 1984 through 1986 Hernandez was a model of consistency at bat, hitting between .309 and .311 during those three seasons.

Hernandez's intelligence, drive, and team leadership were recognized, and he was named the Mets team captain in 1987. Injuries hit Keith Hernandez in 1988, a hamstring shelved him for much of the 1988 season, and knee problems laid him low in 1989. He was released by the Mets at the end of the season. Hernandez signed with Cleveland and played sparingly with the Indians where he hit .200 in his last season in the major leagues.

In his career that spanned seventeen years, Hernandez left the game with a .298 career batting average and 161 home runs.

JESSE OROSCO

Still going strong in the 2001 season with the Los Angeles Dodgers, Jesse Orosco is one of the few players in the history of Major League Baseball to toil in four decades.

The Mets got Jesse Orosco from the Minnesota Twins in December 1978 in the Jerry Koosman trade. By 1983 Orosco was the Mets' top closer. In 1983 Orosco showed baseball what he could do as a reliever by winning 13 games in addition to his 13 saves, and posted an ERA of 1.48.

The left-hander saved 31 games in the 1984, and after that season he began sharing closer duties with the right-hander Roger McDowell. In the 1985 and 1986 seasons Orosco had 38 saves, and in the 1986 NLCS against the Astros he set a playoff record with three wins. In a gutsy performance he got Houston outfielder Kevin Bass for the final out in the marathon sixteen-inning sixth game of the series. In the World Series against the Red Sox, Orosco continued to shine, saving Games Four and Seven. Mets fans still remember the jubilant image of Orosco falling to his knees on the mound and throwing his glove in the air after striking out Red Sox Marty Barrett to end the Series.

Jesse Orosco was traded to the Dodgers at the end of the 1987 season. It was rumored the 1986 NLCS and World Series hero had a tender elbow. Since then he has pitched as a closer and set-up man for the Dodgers, Indians, Brewers, Orioles, and Cardinals. His best season since his trade was in 1997 when he pitched in 71 games for the Baltimore Orioles and posted an ERA of 2.32.

In 1999 Orosco broke Hoyt Whilhelm's record for most appearances on the mound.

Orosco was traded back to the Mets after his record-setting year of 1999 but the Mets sent him off to St. Louis for Joe McEwing.

DARRYL STRAWBERRY

Darryl Strawberry was going to be the Golden Boy of New York Baseball. The Los Angeles native came up to the Mets during the 1983 season and during his eight-year career with the team his accomplishments were many. Sadly as in the case of his Mets teammate and friend Dwight Gooden, drugs and alcohol curtailed what could have been a Hall of Fame career.

Strawberry was the Mets number-one pick in the 1980 draft and he signed with them from Los Angeles' Crenshaw High School. Some called the eighteen-year-old prospect a "Black Ted Williams." Three years after signing, Darryl Strawberry was with the New York Mets.

The twenty-one-year-old Strawberry hit 26 home runs and knocked in 74 runs in 117 games his rookie year, but bigger seasons were to follow. The next two years Strawberry hit 56 home runs and knocked in 176 runs. His home runs were often tape-measure shots, and Mets watchers can recall how everything would stop when the young slugger stepped up to the plate in anticipation of another Strawberry blast.

Strawberry hit 27 home runs and brought in 93 runs with the 1986 Championship team. In that year's NLCS, Strawberry struck out 12 times on 22 at bats, but his three-run homer gave the Mets a 6–5 win in Game Three. He also hit the game-tying home run in New York's 2–1 win over Nolan Ryan in Game Five. Strawberry had a quiet World Series with his only RBI coming on a home run in Game Seven.

Strawberry's career blossomed in 1987 with 39 home runs, 104 RBIs, and a .284 batting average. He matched his home run numbers in 1988 and again went over the 100 RBI mark.

The following year was an off-season for Strawberry as he hit only 27 home runs and had a .225 batting average. He rebounded in 1990 with 37 home runs and 108 RBIs, but at the end of the year Strawberry signed a five-year contract with the Los Angeles Dodgers.

Though he was erratic on the field, and was accused by some of not hustling, Mets fans mourned the loss of their slugger. But there were also off-field problems with Strawberry. He had run-ins with Davey Johnson, and in 1989 he slugged teammate Keith Hernandez during a team photo session.

The next decade has seen Darryl Strawberry awash in a world of turmoil, controversy, alcoholism, drug abuse, and illness. His career with the Dodgers was less than distinguished and was sandwiched between problems with the IRS for failing to report income, and his drug abuse problems. On April 8, 1994, Strawberry checked himself into the Betty Ford Clinic for substance abuse, a month later the former Mets golden boy was released by the Dodgers.

Strawberry was signed a month later by the Giants but once again had problems. He was suspended for 60 days by baseball for violation of its drug policy and was released by the Giants the same day.

Strawberry's luck turned from bad to worse in February 1995 when he was indicted by the IRS for tax evasion. Strawberry was sentenced to a six-month home confinement and fined $350,000 in back taxes and penalties.

The Yankees signed Darryl Strawberry in 1996 and he contributed to the Bronx Bombers' Championship season with 11 home runs and a .262 batting average in 63 games.

A knee injury put Strawberry on the shelf for the 1997 season but he returned strong in 1998. In only limited play, Strawberry blasted 24 home runs but his season was cut short when he was diagnosed with colon cancer. Strawberry had the cancerous tumor removed that October and doctors were optimistic.

While still battling cancer Strawberry was arrested in Tampa in April 1999 for soliciting a prostituite and drug possession. Once again, he was suspended by baseball, this time for 120 days. Strawberry rejoined the Yankees in early August and he hit .327 with 3 home runs in spot duty.

Darryl Strawberry's last season in the major leagues was 1999. Since the end of that season the former Mets hero continued to battle cancer and his recurring drug problems. In February 2000 Strawberry received a lifetime suspension from baseball for the third positive drug test for cocaine, and in October 2000 he was arrested after leaving a treatment center following a weekend-long drug binge.

Darryl Strawberry hit 335 home runs with a .259 career batting average in the major leagues. Strawberry is also the Mets all-time home run hitter with 252.

ROGER MCDOWELL

The lefty–righty combo of Orosco and McDowell gave the Mets two of the most potent closers in the mid- to late-'80s.

McDowell came to the Mets in the spring of the 1985 and the right-hander compiled a 6–5 record with 17 saves. A noted prankster in the Mets clubhouse, he once set off firecrackers by the bat rack to "wake up the bats." The Ohio native won 14 games which was tops for a reliever, and saved 22 games in 1986.

During 1987 and 1988 McDowell continued to be one of the top relievers in the National League saving 43 games while sharing closer duties with Jesse Orosco and Randy Myers.

Roger McDowell was traded to Philadelphia and then Los Angeles in July 1991 and would remain with the team until 1994. After refusing a minor league assignment, he signed with the Texas Rangers. McDowell's once lethal sinker was no longer sinking, but his career was. Though he signed with the Orioles in 1996 shoulder injuries shortened his season. McDowell attempted a comeback with the White Sox in 1988 but due to continued shoulder problems decided to call it quits.

Over McDowell's 12-year career he won 70 games and lost 70, with 159 saves, and an ERA of 3.30.

KEVIN MCREYNOLDS

When he signed with the San Diego Padres as the sixth player taken in the June 1981 draft Kevin McReynolds had a "can't miss" label. The Arkansas native possessed power, speed, and defensive skills for superstardom in the big leagues.

He made it up to the Padres in 1983 and by their pennant winning year of 1984 was the team's starting center fielder. In his first full season, McReynolds hit .278, with 20 home runs, and 75 RBIs but the following year he slumped, hitting only .234. He rebounded in 1986 hitting .288 with 26 home runs.

Kevin McReynolds was traded to the Mets on December 12, 1986, for Kevin Mitchell, outfielders Stan Jefferson and Shawn Abner, and two minor leaguers. San Diego also threw in pitcher Gene Walter.

McReynolds compiled good numbers with the Mets in 1987. He hit .276, with 26 home runs, and 95 RBIs, and over the next two seasons McReynolds averaged .279, with 49 home runs and 184 RBIs. Despite putting up those respectable numbers, being one the of the National League's top left fielders, and stealing 21 bases in 1988 without being thrown out, McReynolds was never a fan favorite. Met fans complained that he didn't hit with men on base and was often prone to long slumps.

The Mets traded Kevin McReynolds to Kansas City along with infielder Gregg Jefferies for pitcher Bret Saberhagen. Shoulder injuries hobbled McReynolds in the American League.

McReynolds returned back to the Mets in 1994 and split time in center field with John Cangelosi but neck and knee injuries kept him out of the lineup and McReynolds retired at season's end.

In his 12-year career Kevin McReynolds was a lifetime .265 hitter with 211 home runs.

DAVID CONE

David Cone was arguably the most dominant pitcher in the Mets rotation in the late '80s and early '90s. The Kansas City native topped the NL in strikeouts in 1990 and 1991. His 20–3 season in 1988 helped steamroll the Mets to the top of the NL East.

David Cone originally signed with his hometown team, the Kansas City Royals. He came up to the Royals in 1986 and pitched in 11 games with no decisions. The pitching-rich Royals traded Cone to the Mets in March 1987 for catcher Ed Hearn in a trade that Royals owner Ewing Kaufmann called, "The worst trade in team history."

Cone joined the Mets that spring but a broken finger hampered him during the season as he posted only a 5–6 record, and a 3.71 ERA.

Cone's breakout year came in 1988 as the twenty-five-year-old finished with a 20–3 record and was a strong candidate for the Cy Young Award. With his 90-plus-mph fastball, and a variety of other pitches that he threw at various speeds, David Cone was the scourge of National League hitters.

Cone continued to pitch well for the declining Mets team during the 1989–1991 seasons going 42–32 and leading the NL in strikeouts twice during those three years. On September 10, 1991, Cone tied an NL record—since broken by Kerry Wood of the Cubs—by striking out 19 Philadelphia Phillies in a 9-inning game.

David Cone was a favorite of the fans and media in New York.

Always accessible for an interview, the articulate and engaging Cone would often play basketball with the press at a local YMCA, and was also known as a prankster. Cone would put various celebrities' names on his daily pass list such as Vanna White and Elvis Presley even though they may have been deceased or he had never met them.

The Mets traded Cone to Toronto despite having a 13–7 record, and an ERA of 2.88, for outfielder Ryan Thompson and second baseman Jeff Kent.

Cone contributed to the 1992 Toronto team that went on to win the World Series that year. At season's end Cone was a free agent and decided to return home.

He signed an $18-million contract with the Kansas City Royals. Getting little run support from the light-hitting Royals, Cone finished 11–14 in 1993.

During the strike-shortened season of 1994 Cone took the AL Cy Young Award with 16 wins and an ERA of 2.94. He also pitched three consecutive shutouts, and had 28 straight scoreless innings, setting a Royals record.

Cone returned to Toronto for the 1995 season, after the Royals refused to pay Cone's hefty salary another year. Toronto didn't hang on to Cone too long that summer either, and he was traded to the Yankees for two minor league players.

As a Yankee, Cone was an integral part of a pitching staff that won four World Championships from 1996 to 2000. But, despite his four World Series rings David Cone's finest moment as a Yankee came on July 18, 1999.

Perhaps it was fate that Don Larsen—who threw the immortal no-hitter against the Brooklyn Dodgers in the 1956 World Series—threw out the first pitch that day at Yankee Stadium. Joining baseball's select club, David Cone pitched that baseball rarity, a perfect game, against the Montreal Expos.

David Cone left the Yankees after to the 2000 season and in 2001 was active with the Boston Red Sox.

JOHN FRANCO

Despite being the set-up guy for Armando Benitez during the past two seasons, John Franco remains the Mets all-time save leader, and has appeared in more games than any Mets pitcher.

The Brooklyn native and Lafayette High School grad also pitched for the St. John's University team where as a freshman he pitched two no-hitters.

John Franco made his major league debut with the Cincinnati Reds in 1984 and by 1986 he was their top closer. Franco made the NL All-Star teams in 1986 and 1987, saving 61 games in 73 chances. The following two seasons Franco was even more prolific saving 71 games in 79 chances.

The Mets and the Reds swapped their top closers when the Mets sent Randy Myers to Cincinnati for Franco, and in 1990 he returned home to New York.

Franco picked up where he had left off in Cincinnati, becoming New York's top fireman during the '90s. In that decade Franco saved 268 games in 326 save opportunities.

Franco retires hitters with his guile as a pitcher, rather than with an overpowering fastball. He is a fierce competitor and team leader, as well as a fan favorite. Franco is the second player in big league history to record over 400 saves. Towards the tail-end of the 2001 season John Franco has collected 422 saves during his 18-year career.

John Franco lives with his family on Staten Island and is active in community activities and charities.

TODD HUNDLEY

The son of former major league catcher Randy Hundley, Todd Hundley also found his calling behind the plate. Hundley caught 745 games for the Mets from 1990 until his trade to the Dodgers in 1998. Hundley's total is the second highest in club history eclipsed only by Jerry Grote who caught 1,176 games.

Hundley's top seasons with the Mets were his All-Star years of 1996 and 1997. In those two years the switch-hitting Hundley hit 71 home runs, and knocked in 200 runs. His 41 home runs in 1996 established a major league record for most home runs hit by a catcher in a season. The 41 home runs hit by Hundley in 1996 also topped Darryl Strawberry's 1988 team record of 39.

Hundley fought a shoulder injury that put him out for a large part of the 1998 season. With the arrival of Mike Piazza that year Hundley's days as the Mets catcher came to an end. He tried playing left field but the position was a mystery to him.

There was also bad blood between manager Bobby Valentine and Hundley and he was traded to the Los Angles Dodgers in December 1998. He suffered a wrist injury in 1999 and hit only .207 with 24 home runs. Hundley came back strong in 2000 hitting .284 with 24 home runs.

2001 saw free agent Todd Hundley sign a contract with the Chicago Cubs. Hundley returned to Wrigley Field where his father had caught eight season for the Chicago Cubs.

EDGARDO ALFONZO

Due to injuries, 2001 was an off-season for the Mets all-time top-hitting second baseman. He finished the season hitting only .243, with 17 home runs.

Alfonzo came up to the Mets in the 1995 as a twenty-two-year-old rookie and hit .278 for the year. The Venezuelan native has deep Met roots; his brother Roberto was an infielder in the Mets farm system in 1993–1994, and his brother Edgar managed the Mets minor league Brooklyn Cyclones in 2001.

Alfonzo has put up very impressive numbers since becoming a

Met. In 1997, his third season in the bigs, he hit .315 with 10 home runs, showing that he was legitimate big league hitter. From 1998 through 2000 his batting average was .302 with a total of 69 home runs.

Coming off the back and finger injuries that hampered him during 2001, big things are anticipated of the Mets second baseman in the 2002 season.

MIKE PIAZZA

Often called the greatest hitting catcher in modern baseball, Mike Piazza came to the Mets in a trade with the Florida Marlins on May 22, 1998, for outfielder Preston Wilson (Mookie's stepson), and pitcher Ed Yarnell. Mets fans rejoiced as Piazza was the biggest superstar the team had ever acquired.

The road to the big leagues was not easy for the Norristown, Pennsylvania, native. Piazza was a sixty-second-round draft pick of the Los Angeles Dodgers in 1988; the 1,390 player selected. On top of that, many felt he was only taken by the Dodgers because of his father's longtime friendship with manager Tommy Lasorda.

It took Piazza four seasons to make it to Los Angeles and when he came up to the majors he came up in a big way. In his rookie season Piazza batted .318, blasted 35 home runs, and had 112 RBIs. He took the National League Rookie of the Year Award.

Piazza continued to have All-Star seasons every year he was in Los Angeles between 1994 and 1996 as he hit between .319 and .346. He hit 24 home runs in the strike-shortened season of 1994, 32 in 1995, and 38 in 1996.

Mike Piazza reached his zenith as a Dodger in 1997 having perhaps the finest season at the plate a catcher has ever had. In 1997 Piazza hit .362, with 40 home runs, and 124 RBIs.

The Dodgers, fearing they didn't have the cash to sign Piazza to a new contract, made a major deal on May 15, 1998, sending their All-Star catcher and future Met Todd Zeile to the Florida Marlins for outfielder Gary Sheffield, catcher Charlie Johnson, and outfielder Jim Eisenreich.

Piazza's stay in Florida was short-lived. Just one week later he joined the Mets and fans rejoiced as it was felt that Piazza was the guy who would drive the Mets bus back to the pennant.

Despite an early slump with the Mets, Piazza returned to form and ended the season hitting a sizzling .328, with 32 home runs. Shortly after the 1998 season the Mets rewarded him with a seven-year contract worth $91 million.

In 1999 Piazza helped the Mets to their first postseason appearance in eleven years. Piazza had a fine season and hit .303 with 40 home runs and 124 RBIs.

Piazza once again lead the Mets charge in 2000, and was the team's leading hitter going into the World Series with a .324 batting average, 38 home runs, and 113 RBIs during the season.

That year Piazza had a 15-game RBI streak, and on April 14, against the Pirates he had five hits in a twelve-inning game, including a double and two home runs.

2001 was a slightly subpar year for the thirty-three-year-old Piazza, although he still led the team hitting .300, with 36 home runs.

Many fans feel Piazza's career will be lengthened if he moves from behind the plate to possibly play first base. No matter where he plays, Mike Piazza is destined for Cooperstown and is the finest hitter the Mets have ever had.

AL LEITER

The ace of the Mets pitching staff, Al Leiter has led the Mets in wins every season since the 1998 season when he came over from the Florida Marlins. That year he posted his top season in the bigs with a 17–6 record.

Drafted by the Yankees in the second round of the 1984 draft, Leiter was considered by Yankees as their next great arm. Injuries hampered the left-hander in the early part of his career. Leiter came up in 1987 and had a record of 2–2 with a high 6.35 ERA. But, the pitching shortage on the Yankees put the New Jersey native in their starting rotation for the 1988 season. A continuing blister problem often took him out of the rotation that year. The Yankees traded him to Toronto in the early part of the 1989 season.

Injuries continued to plague Leiter in Canada from 1989 to 1992 and he appeared in only nine games for the Blue Jays. During those years Leiter had arthroscopic surgery twice, an irritated nerve in his left elbow, and tendinitis.

In 1993 Al Leiter began earning his paycheck as he compiled a 9–6 record for the Blue Jays as they won their second consecutive World Series.

A healthy Al Leiter won 11 games for the Toronto in 1995, striking out 153, and posting a very respectable 3.64 ERA. But, in December 1995, he signed a contract with the fledgling Florida Marlins.

The following season was a memorable one for Leiter as he won 16 games. But, even more outstanding was the no-hitter he threw against the Colorado Rockies on May 11, 1996, in an 11–0 Florida win. Leiter also appeared in the All-Star Game as a closer in a NL win.

Al Leiter's last season in Florida would be 1997. He put in a 11–9 record with the Marlins, and though he didn't get a decision in the Marlins' World Series victory over the Cleveland Indians, Leiter pitched six strong innings in Game Seven, giving up only two runs. The Marlins would take the game in the eleventh inning and beat Cleveland 3–2.

The Marlins cleaned house after their World Series to bring down the payroll, and Leiter was traded to the Mets for minor league pitcher A. J. Burnett.

Since 1998, Leiter has been the ace of the Mets starting rotation. His 16 wins were tops on the Mets pennant-winning 2000 team, and his gritty performance in Game Five of the 2000 World Series when he threw 142 pitches in the Mets loss, won Leiter the admiration of baseball fans throughout the country.

Al Leiter is a star off the field as well and he has been a generous financial supporter of many charities. After he signed his $32 million contract in 1998, Leiter publicly pledged to donate one million dollars to children's charities. He has established "Leiter's Landing," an organization to help needy children, and donated $100,000 to build a baseball field in his hometown of Toms River, New Jersey.

ARMANDO BENITEZ

The latest in the fine line of Met closers is Armando Benitez. Benitez is the all-time Met seasonal save leader with 43 saves in the 2001 season.

The fireballing Dominican came to the Mets at the end of 1998 from Baltimore. As an Oriole, Benitez served mainly as a set-up man. In the 1997 season Benitez allowed only 49 hits in 73.3 innings, and struck out 106 batters, but Orioles brass felt the 6-foot-4, 230-pound pitcher lacked maturity and lapses in concentration. It was felt Benitez took more pride in intimidating batters than getting them out.

Coming over to the Mets for the 1999 season, Benitez succeeded John Franco as the Mets closer in July. Benitez enjoyed a fine 1999 season winning 4 games and losing 3 and saving 22 games while posting a 1.85 ERA.

Despite having a fine season in 2000 and setting a then-Met record of 41 saves in a season, Benitez struggled in postseason play. In the NL divisional series against the Giants, Benitez surrendered a game-tying home run to J. T. Snow in the ninth inning of

Game Two. Although the Mets would win the game in extra innings, his troubles continued in the World Series as he blew a save opportunity in Game One that the Yankees would win in the twelfth inning.

In the off-season Armando Benitez is a rancher with a 1,000-acre ranch in his native Dominican Republic. At twenty-nine Benitez figures to be the Mets closer for a number of years.

Mets Stats: Top Three

METS ALL-TIME BATTING LEADERS 1962–2001

Average
1. John Olerud 1997–1999 .315
2. Mike Piazza 1998–2001 .313
3. Keith Hernandez 1983–1989 .297

At Bats
1. Ed Kranepool 1962–1979 5,436
2. Bud Harrelson 1965–1977 4,390
3. Cleon Jones 1963–1975 4,223

Base Hits
1. Ed Kranepool 1962–1979 1,418
2. Cleon Jones 1963–1975 1,188
3. Mookie Wilson 1980–1989 1,112

Extra Base Hits
1. Darryl Strawberry 1983–1990 469

2. Howard Johnson 1985–1993   424
3. Ed Kranepool 1962–1979   368

Home Runs

1. Darryl Strawberry 1983–1990   252
2. Howard Johnson 1985–1993   192
3. Dave Kingman 1975–1977 & 1981–1983   154

Doubles

1. Ed Kranepool 1962–1979   225
2. Howard Johnson 1985–1993   214
3. Darryl Strawberry 1983–1990   187

Triples

1. Mookie Wilson 1980–1989   62
2. Bud Harrelson 1965–1977   45
3. Cleon Jones 1963–1975   33

Total Bases

1. Ed Kranepool 1962–1979   2,047
2. Darryl Strawberry 1983–1990   2,028
3. Howard Johnson 1985–1993   1,823

RBIs

1. Darryl Strawberry 1983–1990   733
2. Howard Johnson 1985–1993   629
3. Ed Kranepool 1962–1979   614

Stolen Bases

1. Mookie Wilson 1980–1989   281
2. Howard Johnson 1985–1993   202
3. Darryl Strawberry 1983–1990   191

Runs Scored

1. Darryl Strawberry 1983–1990   662
2. Howard Johnson 1985–1993   627
3. Mookie Wilson 1980–1989   592

Pinch Hits

1. Ed Kranepool 1962–1979   90
2. Rusty Staub 1972–1975 & 1981–1985 77
3. Gil Hodges 1962–1963 & Matt Franco 1996–2000 48

Hit by Pitch

1. Ron Hunt 1963–1966   44
2. Cleon Jones 1963–1975   39
3. Felix Millan 1973–1977   36

Games Played

1. Ed Kranepool 1962–1979   1,853
2. Bud Harreslon 1965–1977   1,322
3. Jerry Grote 1966–1977   1,235

METS SEASON HITTING LEADERS

Batting Average

1. John Olerud 1998   .354
2. Cleon Jones 1969   .340
3. Lance Johnson 1996   .333

At Bats

1. Lance Johnson 1996   682
2. Felix Millan 1975   676
3. Mookie Wilson 1982   639

Base Hits
1. Lance Johnson 1996   227
2. John Olerud 1998   197
3. Edgardo Alfonzo 1998 & Felix Millan 1975   191

Extra Base Hits
1. Howard Johnson 1989   80
2. Bernard Gilkey 1996   77
3. Howard Johnson 1991   76

Home Runs
1. Todd Hundley 1996   41
2. Mike Piazza 1999   40
3. Darryl Strawberry 1987   39

Doubles
1. Bernard Gilkey 1996   44
2. Howard Johnson 1989   41
3. Edgardo Alfonzo 2000   40

Triples
1. Lance Johnson 1996   21
2. Mookie Wilson 1984   10
3. Charlie Neal 1962   9

Slugging Percentage
1. Mike Piazza 2000   .614
2. Darryl Strawberry 1987   .583
3. Mike Piazza 1999   .575

Total Bases
1. Lance Johnson 1996   327
2. Bernard Gilkey 1996   321
3. Howard Johnson 1989   319

RBIs

1. Mike Piazza 1999   124
2. Bernard Gilkey 1996 & Howard Johnson 1991   117
3. Mike Piazza 2000   113

Runs Scored

1. Edgardo Alfonzo 1999   123
2. Lance Johnson 1996   117
3. Edgardo Alfonzo 2000   109

Stolen Bases

1. Roger Cedeño 1999   66
2. Mookie Wilson 1982   58
3. Mookie Wilson 1983   54

Walks

1. John Olerud 1999   125
2. Darryl Strawberry 1987 & Keith Hernandez 1984   97
3. John Olerud 1998   95

Games Played

1. John Olerud 1999   162
2. Felix Millan 1975   162
3. Robin Ventura 1999   161

METS' ALL-TIME CAREER PITCHING LEADERS 1962–2001

Most Wins

1. Tom Seaver 1967–1977, 1983   198
2. Dwight Gooden 1984–1994   157
3. Jerry Koosman 1967–1978   140

Most Losses

1. Jerry Koosman 1967–1978	137
2. Tom Seaver 1967– 1977, 1983	124
3. Dwight Gooden 1984–1994	85

Base Hits Allowed

1. Tom Seaver 1967–1977, 1983	2,431
2. Jerry Koosman 1967–1978	2,281
3. Dwight Gooden 1984–1994	1,898

ERA (500 innings pitched)

1. Tom Seaver 1967–1977, 1983	2.57
2. Jesse Orosco 1979, 1981–1987	2.74
3. Jon Matlack 1971–1977	3.03

Game Appearances

1. John Franco 1990–present	605
2. Tom Seaver 1967–1977, 1983	401
3. Jerry Koosman 1967–1978	376

Complete Games

1. Tom Seaver 1967–1977, 1983	171
2. Jerry Koosman 1967–1978	108
3. Dwight Gooden 1984–1994	67

Innings Pitched

1. Tom Seaver 1967–1977, 1983	3,045.0
2. Jerry Koosman 1967–1978	2,545.0
3. Dwight Gooden 1984–1994	2,169.2

Strikeouts

1. Tom Seaver 1967–1977, 1983	2,541
2. Dwight Gooden 1984–1994	1,875
3. Jerry Koosman 1967–1978	1,799

Walks

1. Tom Seaver 1967–1977, 1983   847
2. Jerry Koosman 1967–1978   820
3. Dwight Gooden 1984–1994   651

Shutouts

1. Tom Seaver 1967–1977, 1983   44
2. Jerry Koosman 1967–1978 &
   Jon Matlack 1971–1977   26
3. Dwight Gooden 1984–1994   23

Saves

1. John Franco 1990–present   274
2. Jesse Orosco 1979, 1981–1987   107
3. Tug McGraw 1965–1967, 1969–1974   85

Starts

1. Tom Seaver 1967–1977, 1983   395
2. Jerry Koosman 1967–1978   346
3. Dwight Gooden 1984–1994   303

METS SEASON PITCHING LEADERS 1962–2001

Most Wins

1. Tom Seaver 1969   25
2. Dwight Gooden 1985   24
3. Tom Seaver 1975   22

Most Losses

1. Roger Craig 1962 & Jack Fisher 1965   24
2. Roger Craig 1963   22
3. Al Jackson 1962   20

Runs Allowed

1. Roger Craig 1962	117
2. Jack Fisher 1967 & Jay Hook 1962	115
3. Al Jackson 1962	113

ERA

1. Dwight Gooden 1985	1.53
2. Tom Seaver 1971	1.76
3. Tom Seaver 1973	2.08

Game Appearances

1. Turk Wendell 1999	80
2. Armando Benitez 1999	77
3. Turk Wendell 2000	77

Starts

1. Jack Fisher 1965	36
2. Tom Seaver 1970	36
3. Tom Seaver 1973	36

Complete Games

1. Tom Seaver 1971	21
2. Tom Seaver 1970	19
3. Tom Seaver 1967	18

Innings Pitched

1. Tom Seaver 1970	291.0
2. Tom Seaver 1973	290.0
3. Tom Seaver 1971	286.0

Strikeouts

1. Tom Seaver 1971   289
2. Tom Seaver 1970   283
3. Dwight Gooden 1984   276

Walks

1. Nolan Ryan 1968   116
2. Ron Darling 1985   115
3. Mike Torrez 1983   113

Hits Allowed

1. Roger Craig 1962   261
2. Frank Viola 1991   259
3. Jerry Koosman 1974   258

Runs Allowed

1. Jay Hook 1962   137
2. Roger Craig 1962   133
3. Al Jackson 1962   132

Shutouts

1. Dwight Gooden 1985   8
2. Jerry Koosman 1968 & Jon Matlack 1974 7
3. Jerry Koosman 1969   6

Saves

1. Armando Benitez 2000   43
2. Armando Benitez 2001   41
3. John Franco 1997   36

Mets Trivia

OH, THOSE EARLY YEARS!

1. Why did the Mets choose orange and blue as their colors?
2. Who was the Mets first manager in their first season?
3. In what Stadium did the Mets play their first two seasons?
4. Which former Brooklyn Dodger slugger joined the Mets in 1963?
5. Name the Hall of Fame outfielder who played for the "Amazins" in 1962.
6. He clouted 34 homers for the Mets in their first season and was also hit by pitches twice in one inning. Who was he?
7. He played first base and later managed the Mets to their first world championship. Who was he?
8. He lost 20 games in the Mets' first season. This former Dodgers and Mets hurler later managed the San Diego Padres in the late '70s, and San Francisco Giants from 1985–1992. Who was he?
9. Name the other expansion team that entered the National League with the Mets in 1962.

10. How many games did the Mets lose in 1962?

11. Who was the Mets outfielder who ran around the bases backwards after hitting his 100th career homer?

12. He came to the Mets in 1963, hit .273 as a rookie, and would blossom into an All-Star the following season. Who was he?

13. Name the New York City schoolboy phenom who signed with the Mets in 1962 and played with them through 1979.

14. True or false: The Mets had three 20-game losers in their inaugural season.

15. Who was the baseball legend who once hit a record .424 in 1924 and was a Mets coach in 1962?

16. He pitched for the Mets in the 1963 and 1964 seasons, but is best known for serving Roger Maris the pitch that led to his 61st home run in 1961. Who was he?

17. True or false: Yogi Berra played for the Mets in 1965.

18. Who replaced Casey Stengel as the Mets' skipper in 1965?

19. With what other New York major league teams was Casey Stengel associated?

20. Name the Mets original television broadcasting team.

21. What Milwaukee Braves Hall of Fame pitcher pitched for the Mets in 1965?

22. Name the catcher whose nickname was "Choo Choo".

23. Following his first selection in the expansion draft that stocked the Mets with players for the 1962 season, Casey Stengel said, "Without a catcher, you'll have a lot of passed balls." So the Mets recruited which veteran big league catcher?
    A: Harry Chiti
    B: Jerry Grote
    C: Hobie Landrith

      D: Joe Torre

      E: Joe Ginsberg

24. Who was the first regular season opponent the Mets faced in their first game played on April 11, 1962?

      A: the Giants

      B: the Cardinals

      C: the Dodgers

      D: the Braves

      E: the Cubs

25. Which player had the first hit for the Mets in their opening game in 1962?

      A: Gil Hodges

      B: Richie Ashburn

      C: Gus Bell

      D: Elio Chacon

      E: Marv Throneberry

26. Which veteran National League star hit the first home run for the Mets?

      A: Richie Ashburn

      B: Felix Mantilla

      C: Charlie Neal

      D: Gil Hodges

      E: Frank Thomas

27. Name the Mets pitcher who threw four shutouts in the 1963 season.

      A: Al Jackson

      B: Carlton Willey

      C: Roger Craig

      D: Tom Seaver

      E: Tracy Stallard

28. The Mets lost a twenty-three-inning game in 1964 to which team?

      A: the Giants

B: the Astros

C: the Phillies

D: the Cubs

29. What 1962 ballplayer's initials spelled MET?

30. Who hit the first home run at Shea Stadium in April 1964?

    A: Frank Thomas

    B: Frank Howard

    C: Willie Stargell

    D: Pete Rose

    E: Willie Mays

    F: Frank Robinson

31. In what year did the Mets finally make it out of the NL cellar? (Hint: It was also the season they lost less than 100 games).

    A: 1963

    B: 1964

    C: 1965

    D: 1969

    E: 1966

32. What year was Tom Seaver's rookie season?

33. Which former Dodgers outfielder led the Mets in hitting during the 1967 season?

34. Who threw a perfect game against the Mets on June 22, 1964?

    A: Jim Bunning

    B: Sandy Koufax

    C: Juan Marichal

    D: Bob Gibson

    E: Coot Veale

35. How many wins did Tom Seaver have in his rookie season?

    A: 9

B: 20

C: 11

D: 16

E: 13

36. What twenty-year-old player joined the Mets in 1965 and played shortstop for them for the next twelve years?

37. What team did Gil Hodges manage before returning to New York to handle the Mets?

38. When did Gil Hodges return to New York to manage the Mets?

39. What nineteen-year-old made his Mets debut in 1966 and fanned six in the three innings he pitched?

A: Nolan Ryan

B: Jerry Koosman

C: Tug McGraw

D: Dennis Ribant

E: Jim Bethke

F: Gary Gentry.

40. Name the beer company that sponsored the Mets in their early years.

41. Name the Mets first owner.

42. What was Casey Stengel's jersey number? (Hint: It is one of only four retired by the Mets.)

BUILDING SOMETHING AND THE MIRACLE AT FLUSHING MEADOWS

1. What stalwart southpaw pitched for the Mets from 1967 through 1978 and chalked up 222 major league wins?

2. The Mets traded Tommy Davis and Al Weis to the White Sox for which outfielder at the end of the 1967 season?

3. What was Gil Hodges's jersey number as a Brooklyn Dodger and later as the Mets manager?

4. The Mets lost a 24-inning, 1–0 game to which team in April 1968?

    A: the Expos

    B: the Dodgers

    C: the Braves

    D: the Astros

    E: the Pirates

5. What year did divisional play begin in the National League?

6. Montreal and San Diego joined the National League in what year?

    A: 1969

    B: 1972

    C: 1966

    D: 1970

    (FMI: What does this have to do with the Mets?)

7. What former Pirates and Red Sox slugging first baseman played briefly for the Mets in 1966?

8. What infielder played for the Mets from 1967–1968 and got into a row with Yogi Berra for playing a harmonica on the Yankees team bus?

9. Catcher Jerry Grote came from which team?

    A: the Yankees

    B: the Braves

    C: the Tigers

    D: the Astros

    E: the Dodgers

10. What right-handed hitting first baseman was picked up by the Mets from Montreal for the 1969 pennant run?

11. What was Cleon Jones's batting average in 1969?

    A: .325

    B: .299

C: .354

D: .340

E: .308

12. What leading NL East team did the Mets overtake for the 1969 pennant?

A: the Pirates

B: the Cubs

C: the Phillies

D: the Cardinals.

13. Which Cardinal pitcher struck out 19 Mets in a 1969 game but still lost 4–3 as Ron Swoboda belted two home runs?

14. How many of their final 49 games did the Mets win in 1969?

A: 42

B: 35

C: 38

D: 40

15. How many games did Tom Seaver win in 1969?

A: 25

B: 19

C: 22

D: 16

E: 21

16. Whose nickname was "The Franchise?"

A: Tommie Agee

B: Tom Seaver

C: Ed Kranepool

D: Cleon Jones

D: Tug McGraw

17. Which Chicago Cub broke up Tom Seaver's bid for a no-hitter in 1969?

A: Joe Pepitone

B: Ernie Banks

C: Billy Williams

D: Jimmy Qualls

E: Lance Haffner

18. What outfielder did Gil Hodges pull from the game for not hustling?

A: Tommie Agee

B: Cleon Jones

C: Ed Kranepool

D: Ron Swoboda

E: Don Hahn

19. How many games did the Mets win in the 1969 regular season?

A: 89

B: 105

C: 97

D: 100

E: 93

20. Who was the Mets top slugger with 26 home runs in 1969?

A: Ed Kranepool

B: Art Shamsky

C: Ron Swoboda

D: Tommie Agee

21. Who was the solid-hitting, dependable-fielding, second baseman on the '69 Mets?

22. Who was the twenty-one-year-old rookie the Mets had at third base until 1976?

23. Who did the Mets play in the 1969 NL playoffs?

A: the Reds

B: the Dodgers

C: the Braves

D: the Giants

24. True or false: The Mets swept the NL playoffs 3–0 over their NL West opponent in 1969.

25. Who did the Mets face in the 1969 World Series?
    A: the Orioles
    B: the Tigers
    C: the Yankees
    D: the A's
    E: the Red Sox

26. True or false: It took the Mets seven games to win the 1969 World Series.

27. Who won two games in the 1969 World Series?

28. Which light-hitting infielder tied up the last game of the 1969 World Series with a home run in the bottom of the seventh inning?

29. Which Mets outfielder saved Game Three of the 1969 World Series with a desperate sliding catch in the top of the seventh inning?

30. What hitter sent a pop up to Cleon Jones to end 1969 World Series? (Hint: Would later manage the Mets.)

31. Who was the 1969 World Series MVP?
    A: Jerry Koosman
    B: Tommie Agee
    C: Donn Clendenon
    D: Nolan Ryan
    E: Tom Seaver
    F: Wayne Garrett
    G: Al Weis

32. How many games did Nolan Ryan win as a Mets pitcher?
    A: 29
    B: 12
    C: 103
    D: 44
    E: 51

33. His best season in the majors was in 1969 when he finished 13–12 for the Mets. Who was he?

34. Which Mets player was a key cog in the 1969 Mets Championship and had a son who would later play for the Dallas Cowboys?

BETWEEN PENNANTS, 1970–1972 AND YA GOTTA BELIEVE!

1. Where did the Mets finish in 1970?
   A: last
   B: second
   C: third
   D: fifth
   E: fourth
2. He hit .263 and had five home runs with the Mets in 1970, but had his best years as an outfielder with the Expos and the Orioles. Who was he?
3. Name the young outfielder who was traded to Kansas City by the Mets in 1970.
4. In 1970, how many games did Ken Boswell play on second base without committing an error?
   A: 94
   B: 85
   C: 78
   D: 103
5. In an April 1970 game, Tom Seaver struck out how many San Diego Padres?
   A: 19
   B: 18
   C: 16
   D: 15
   E: 21
6. What team was Ron Swoboda traded to after the 1971 season?

A: the Phillies
B: the Expos
C: the Yankees
D: the Astros
E: the Indians

7. Which All-Star infielder did the Mets trade Nolan Ryan for in 1972?

8. After Gil Hodges's death in April 1972 who succeeded him as the Mets manager?

9. What legendary Hall of Fame outfielder returned to New York to play for the Mets in the spring of 1972?

10. Who did the Mets trade Ken Singleton and Tim Foli for in 1972?

11. Name the Met whose nickname was "The Little Hammer"?
    A: Cleon Jones
    B: Tommy Agee
    C: Don Hahn
    D: John Milner

12. Which Mets pitcher served up Roberto Clemente's 3000th and final hit on September 30, 1972?
    A: Buzz Capra
    B: Gary Gentry
    C: Danny Frisella
    D: Jon Matlack
    E: Ray Sadecki

13. The Mets traded pitchers Gary Gentry and Danny Frisella to what team in exchange for George Stone and Felix Millan?
    A: the Cubs
    B: the Texas Rangers
    C: the Brewers
    D: the Braves
    E: the Reds

14. What Mets player is credited with originating the 1973 battle cry "Ya gotta believe"?

    A: Cleon Jones

    B: Tug McGraw

    C: Rusty Staub

    D: Tom Seaver

    E: Willie Mays

15. What was Willie Mays's jersey number that was retired by the Mets?

    A: 24

    B: 5

    C: 7

    D: 35

    E: 42

16. What is Yogi Berra's given name?

17. What veteran third baseman batted .225 in 1971 in his one season with the Mets.

18. Name the Mets outfielder who parlayed his hobby of cooking into a couple of Manhattan restaurants that bore his name.

19. What pitcher did the Mets trade to the San Francisco Giants for Willie Mays in 1972?

20. Name the three National League teams that had better win-loss records than the Mets in 1973.

21. True or false: The Mets had the lowest batting average in the National League during the 1973 season.

22. The Mets won the NL East, and later the National League pennant, in 1973 with the lowest winning percentage of any team in Major League Baseball history. What was the percentage?

    A: .511

    B: .523

    C: .501

D: .509

E: .505.

23. What team finished behind the Mets in the race for the NL East flag in 1973?

A: the Pirates

B: the Expos

C: the Cardinals

D: the Cubs.

24. Who was the Mets home run leader in 1973?

A: John Milner

B: Willie Mays

C: Rusty Staub

D: Joe Torre

E: Ed Kranepool

25. Which Mets player led the team with a .290 batting average in 1973?

A: Cleon Jones

B: Felix Millan

C: Rusty Staub

D: George Theodore

E: Ed Kranepool

26. Who was the Mets opponent in the 1973 National League Championship series?

A: the Dodgers

B: the Astros

C: the Giants

D: the Braves

E: the Reds

27. The wild bench-clearing brawl that took place in the third game of the NLCS started as a fight between Bud Harrelson and who?

28. Name the Mets 1973 World Series opponent?

A: the Tigers

B: the Red Sox

C: the Orioles

D: the A's

E: the Angels

29. Which Mets player drove in the winning run in the twelfth inning of the second game of 1973 World Series?

    A: Willie Mays

    B: Ed Kranepool

    C: Wayne Garrett

    D: Rusty Staub

    E: Cleon Jones

30. Which Mets pitcher gave up only three hits in eight innings in Game Four of the 1973 World Series?

    A: George Stone

    B: Jim McAndrew

    C: Jon Matlack

    D: Jerry Koosman

    E: Tug McGraw

31. Who was the leading Mets hitter in the 1973 World Series with a .423 batting average?

    A: Rusty Staub

    B: Wayne Garrett

    C: Cleon Jones

    D: Willie Mays

    E: Felix Millan

32. What catcher spent twelve years as the Mets backup?

33. Which Mets outfielder's nickname was the "Stork"?

34. Name the pitcher the Mets picked up prior to 1973 who posted a 12–3 record.

35. The Mets acquired Felix Millan from what NL team?

    A: the Expos

    B: the Pirates

    C: the Phillies

    D: the Dodgers

YEARS OF STRUGGLE, 1974–1978

1. How many consecutive seasons did Tom Seaver have with two hundred or more strikeouts?
2. The Mets traded Ray Sadecki to the Cardinals for which solid hitting catcher and third baseman who would later go on to have a distinguished career as a big league manager?
3. Which team was Tug Mcgraw traded to in December 1974?
   A: the Phillies
   B: the Red Sox
   C: the Dodgers
   D: the A's
   E: the Pirates
4. What young catcher would eventually replace the veteran Jerry Grote for the Mets in the mid-seventies?
5. What power hitter did the Mets acquire from San Francisco prior to the 1975 season?
6. In 1975 Tom Seaver won his third Cy Young Award, yet lost nine games. How many wins did he record that season?
7. Yogi Berra was released as Mets manager in August 1975. Who replaced him for the remainder of the season?
8. Who did the Mets name to manage the team for the 1976 season?
9. Who broke Frank Thomas's Mets record of 34 home runs by hitting 36 for the Mets in 1975?
10. Who knocked out 105 runs for the Mets in 1975?
    A: Cleon Jones
    B: Lee Mazzilli
    C: Rusty Staub
    D: Dave Kingman
    E: John Stearns

11. Who was the leading hitter for the Mets in 1975 with a .294 batting average?

    A: Cleon Jones

    B: Rusty Staub

    C: John Milner

    D: Felix Millan

    E: Del Unser.

12. What Mets reliever had a 1.48 ERA in 1975 and would later coach Mets pitchers?

13. Mets fans thought they had a star when this young outfielder came up at the tail-end of the 1975 season and hit .302, who was he?

14. Name the youngest Alou brother who played for the Mets in 1975.

15. Who was the lefty hurler who won twenty-one games for the Mets in 1976?

16. The Mets traded Rusty Staub to the Detroit Tigers for which superb southpaw hurler?

17. Who was Tom Seaver traded to the Cincinnati Reds for in 1977?

18. Who was the chairman of the board who orchestrated the Seaver deal?

19. What player was traded to San Diego for Bobby Valentine and pitcher Paul Siebert?

20. What former first base coach replaced Joe Frazier as the manager of the Mets in 1977?

21. Which veteran American League infielder led the Mets in hits during the 1975 season with a .304 average?

22. What threesome was tied for the most Mets homers in 1977 with 12 apiece?

23. What other NL teams beside the Mets did Joe Torre play for?

24. What Brooklyn high school did Lee Mazzilli attend?

25. Jerry Koosman was traded to what team for two minor league pitchers?
    A: the Pirates
    B: the Astros
    C: the Dodgers
    D: the Twins
    E: the White Sox
26. What slick-fielding first baseman played for the Mets in the late '70s?

THE AGONY CONTINUES, 1978–1983

1. What team was Buddy Harrelson traded to before the 1978 season?
2. What former Yankee outfielder played for the Mets from 1978–1980 but had his career cut short when he tore up his knee tripping over a drainage pipe at Shea Stadium?
3. Which Mets player could play all the outfield positions as well as the infield and led the team in home runs with 16 in 1979?
4. Who was the 1979 pitching ace for the Mets that scored 14 victories for the team?
    A: Pat Zachry
    B: Bob Apodaca
    C: Neil Allen
    D: Craig Swan
    E: Pete Falcone
5. In 1980 the Mets brought in Frank Cashen to run the baseball operations as general manager. What team did Cashen formerly serve in this position?
6. What former Pirates third baseman tied Lee Mazzilli for the most RBIs in 1979?

7. What former teammate of Sandy Koufax from the Lafayette High School baseball team went on to become the owner of the Mets?

8. Which former White Sox outfielder belted three home runs for the Mets in 1980?

9. Who led the Mets staff with ten wins in the 1980 season?

    A: Mark Bomback

    B: Pete Falcone

    C: Neil Allen

    D: Craig Swan

    E: Pat Zachry

10. What Mets player was traded to Montreal in 1981 and became the star of their bullpen?

11. What did Pete Rose set a National League record for in a 1978 game against the Mets at Shea Stadium?

12. Who was the former Orioles pitching coach and Staten Island native that managed the Mets in 1982 and part of 1983?

13. Who signed with the Mets for the 1982 season but had his career year in 1977 with the Reds when he belted 52 home runs?

14. What temperamental slugger joined the Mets for an encore appearance in 1981 and led the National League in home runs with 37 in 1982?

15. What rookie hit .307 for the Mets in 1981?

    A: Keith Hernandez

    B: Hubie Brooks

    C: Darryl Strawberry

    D: Alex Trevino

    E: Lenny Dykstra

16. Name the rookie who swiped twenty-four bases in the 1981 season.

17. Just prior to the 1982 season the Mets traded Lee Mazzilli to the Texas Rangers for two minor league pitchers who made big contributions to the team in later years. Who were they?

18. Which Mets hero rejoined the team in 1983?
    A: Tom Seaver
    B: Jerry Grote
    C: Ed Kranepool
    D: Lee Mazzilli
    E: Jerry Koosman

19. The Mets acquired what veteran right-handed hurler from the Red Sox in 1983?

20. What Mets player took the NL Rookie of the Year Award in 1983?
    A: Dwight Gooden
    B: Len Dykstra
    C: Jesse Orosco
    D: Darryl Strawberry
    E: Ron Darling

21. Who were the two pitchers the Mets traded to St. Louis in 1983 to acquire Keith Hernandez?

22. What former slugger replaced George Bamberger as Mets manager when Bamberger resigned in 1983?

23. What Mets hitter had eight consecutive pinch hits in 1983?

24. Who led the Mets with 28 home runs and 90 RBIs in 1983?
    A: Dave Kingman
    B: Keith Hernandez
    C: Darryl Strawberry
    D: George Foster
    E: Gary Carter

25. Did Keith Hernandez ever win a batting championship?

BUILDING SOMETHING, 1984–1985

1. Who moved up from Tidewater to manage the big club in 1984?

2. What American League team was Tom Seaver picked up by in 1984?
   A: the Yankees
   B: the Orioles
   C: the Red Sox
   D: the Angels
   E: the White Sox

3. The Mets picked up lefty hurler Sid Fernandez from what NL West team?
   A: the Dodgers
   B: the Astros
   C: the Giants
   D: the Padres
   E: the Braves

4. What was Darry Strawberry's jersey number?

5. What was Keith Hernandez's jersey number?

6. What was Keith Hernandez's nickname?

7. What former hoops star from the University of South Carolina was the spot starter and reliever for the Mets in the mid '80s?

8. How many victories did Dwight Gooden record in 1984, his rookie season?
   A: 18
   B: 21
   C: 17
   D: 19
   E: 14

9. Who was the Mets leading hitter with a .311 average in 1984?

    A: Hubie Brooks

    B: Keith Hernandez

    C: Rusty Staub

    D: Mookie Wilson

    E: George Foster

10. Name the 1984 NL Rookie of the Year.

11. Where did the Mets finish in the NL East standings for the 1984 season?

12. The Mets picked up what veteran left-hander from the Cincinnati Reds in 1984?

13. What 1984 Mets hurler would later face the team as a member of the Boston Red Sox in the 1986 World Series?

14. Why did Sid Fernandez choose to wear jersey number 50?

15. Who was the Mets top reliever in 1984 with 31 saves?

    A: Doug Sisk

    B: Wes Gardner

    C: Roger McDowell

    D: Jerry Orosco

    E: Carlos Diaz

16. What was Gary Carter's jersey number?

17. Whose home run during the 1984 season put him in a select group of major leaguers who had hit home runs as a teenager and as a 40-year-old?

18. What team did the Mets acquire Gary Carter from at the end of 1984?

19. The Mets played a memorable nineteen-inning game that the Mets finally won 16–13 against what team on July 4, 1985?

20. The Mets were edged out of the NL East pennant in 1985 by which rival team?

21. How many wins did Dwight Gooden have in 1985, his Cy Young Award–winning year?

A: 27

B: 23

C: 22

D: 24

E: 25

22. What was Dwight Gooden's jersey number?

23. In 1985 Gary Carter's home runs were a record for Mets catchers, before Todd Hundley joined the team. How many did he have?

   A: 29

   B: 32

   C: 34

   D: 40

   E: 35

24. In his initial game with the Mets his home run in the 1985 season opener against Montreal gave the Mets a tenth-inning victory. Who was he?

   A: Gary Carter

   B: Danny Heep

   C: Mookie Wilson

   D: Kevin Mitchell

   E: Len Dykstra

THAT WONDERFUL YEAR, 1986

1. How many games did the Mets win in their 1986 Championship season?

   A: 99

   B: 102

   C: 100

   D: 110

   E: 108

2. The Mets picked up this crafty left-hander from the Red Sox and were rewarded with 18 wins in the 1986 season. Who was he?

3. Five of the Mets made the 1986 National League All-Star team. Who were they?

4. Name the Mets third baseman who had a major comeback year in 1986.

5. Who replaced Mookie Wilson in center field after Wilson's eye injury in the 1986 season?

6. Name the local boy who came "home" for a second stint with the Mets at the mid-point of the 1986 season?

7. Who hit .277 in his rookie season with a dozen home runs playing all the outfield and infield positions with the exception of second base during 1986?

8. The Mets clinched the NL East flag with a 4–2 victory over which NL East foe on September 17, 1986?

9. What was the Mets' lead at the end of the 1986 season?
    A: 18 games
    B: 16 games
    C: 19½ games
    D: 24 games
    E: 21½ games

10. Who was the Mets closest competitor in their division in 1986?

11. Who lead the Mets in wins in the 1986 season?
    A: Sid Fernandez
    B: Bobby Ojeda
    C: Ron Darling
    D: Doc Gooden

12. Who played shortstop for the 1986 Mets?

13. What is Mookie Wilson's given name?

14. Name the two Met bullpen aces who had 43 saves between them.

15. Name the scrappy second baseman who batted .320 in 1986.

16. Who were the Mets opponents in the 1986 NL Championship Series?

17. This former Mets pitcher faced them in the 1986 NLCS and proved to be a major nemesis for the Mets; he also led the NL with 306 strikeouts that year. Who was he?

18. His two-run home run in the 9th inning of the third game in the 1986 NLCS gave the Mets a 6–4 win. Who was he?

    A: Lenny Dykstra

    B: Darryl Strawberry

    C: Ray Knight

    D: Kevin Mitchell

    E: Gary Carter

19. In one of the greatest playoff games in the history of Major League Baseball, the Mets beat the Houston Astros 7–6 taking the National League flag. How many innings did they play?

    A: 19

    B: 17

    C: 13

    D: 16

    E: 20

THE 1986 WORLD SERIES

1. Who was the Mets pitcher in Game One of the 1986 World Series?

    A: Bobby Ojeda

    B: Doc Gooden

    C: Ron Darling

D: Rick Aguilera

E: Roger McDowell

2. Who did the Mets face in the 1986 World Series?

3. Who was the Red Sox manager?

4. Name the Red Sox pitcher, and future Hall of Famer, who missed the 1986 World Series due to a knee injury.

5. Name the player whose miscue in the infield led to the 1–0 Red Sox Game One win in the Series.

6. Name the Red Sox pitcher who shut out the Mets in the first game of the 1986 World Series.

A: Dennis "Oil Can" Boyd

B: Bruce Hurst

C: Bob Stanley

D: Roger Clemens

E: Al Nipper

7. What Yale graduate pitched seven scoreless innings for the Mets in Game Four of the 1986 World Series?

8. Who tied the game by scoring on a wild pitch in the tenth inning of Game Six of the series?

A: Keith Hernandez

B: Wally Backman

C: Kevin Mitchell

D: Ray Knight

E: Rafael Santana

9. Which Red Sox pitcher threw that wild pitch?

A: Dennis "Oil Can" Boyd

B: Calvin Schiraldi

C: Joe Sambito

D: Jeff Sellers

E: Bob Stanley

10. Name the Red Sox first baseman who will be remembered as a World Series goat for allowing Mookie Wil-

son's grounder to go under his glove, giving the Mets the victory in Game Six of the Series?

11. Name the Met who scored the winning run from second base on that first baseman miscue.

    A: Lenny Dykstra

    B: Lee Mazzilli

    C: Stan Jefferson

    D: Ray Knight

    E: Wally Backman

12. Which Mets pitcher started Game Seven in the 1986 Series?

    A: Ron Darling

    B: Roger McDowell

    C: Bobby Ojeda

    D: Dwight Gooden

    E: Sid Fernandez

13. Who was the Red Sox pitcher for that final game?

    A: Roger Clemens

    B: Bruce Hurst

    C: Al Nipper

    D: Dennis "Oil Can" Boyd

    E: Bob Stanley

14. His home run in the bottom of the seventh inning gave the Mets a 4–3 lead in Game Seven. Who was he?

    A: Wally Backman

    B: Ray Knight

    C: Gary Carter

    D: Darryl Strawberry

    E: Mookie Wilson

15. Name the Mets pitcher who threw the last out of the 1986 World Series.

16. Name the Red Sox player who made the final out of the 1986 World Series.

17. Though he wasn't a sports fan, this New York City mayor nonetheless jumped on the Mets' bandwagon and ordered a parade for the World Series heroes after their win in 1986. Who was he?

18. Who was the 1986 Series MVP?
    A: Dwight Gooden
    B: Ray Knight
    C: Keith Hernandez
    D: Mookie Wilson
    E: Gary Carter

CLOSE BUT NO CIGAR 1987–1990

1. Name the San Diego Padres outfielder acquired by the Mets in December of 1986 for Kevin Mitchell and a couple of minor leaguers.

2. His demand for a two-year contract was not met by the Mets and he left New York prior to the 1987 season and signed with the Baltimore Orioles. Who was he?

3. Where did the Mets finish in 1987?

4. Name the Mets player who missed the first month of the 1987 season because of cocaine abuse?

5. Who led the Mets in home runs with 39 and had 104 RBIs in 1987?

6. Name the Mets pitcher acquired from the Kansas City Royals who won only five games for the Mets in 1987, but went on to have an excellent career as a big league hurler?

7. Which hitter for the Mets did the St. Louis Cardinals manager accuse of corking his bat in 1987?

8. What pitcher had a 20–3 mark for the Mets in 1988?
    A: Terry Leach
    B: Dwight Gooden

C: David Cone

D: Sid Fernandez

E: Ron Darling

9. True or false: The Mets bettered their team win record of 108 in a season as they coasted to the NL East flag in 1988.

10. What rookie brought up at the tail-end of the 1988 season had a .321 batting average?

11. Name the Mets foe in the 1988 NLCS.

12. How did the Mets fare in the 1988 NLCS against their Western Division foe?

13. Lenny Dykstra and Roger McDowell were traded to the Phillies in 1989 for which player?

14. The Mets acquired which former 20-game winner from Minnesota in 1989?

15. He belted 36 home runs, knocked in 101 runs, and stole 41 bases for the Mets in 1989. Who was he?

16. The Mets finished second to which team in 1989?

17. What Mets reliever saved 24 games in the 1989 season?

18. Who won 20 games for the Mets in 1990?

    A: Dwight Gooden

    B: David Cone

    C: Sid Fernandez

    D: Ron Darling

    E: Frank Viola

19. The Mets finished in second place in the 1990 NL East race finishing four games out. Who bested them?

    A: Pittsburgh

    B: Chicago

    C: Montreal

    D: Philadelphia

    E: St. Louis

20. He replaced Davey Johnson as the Mets skipper during the 1990 season. Who was he?

21. In 1990 this lefty reliever saved 33 games for the Mets in his first season with the team after coming over from Cincinnati. Who was he?

22. He put up monster numbers with the Mets in 1990, slugging 37 home runs and knocking in 108 runs, but went the free agent route and signed with the L.A. Dodgers in 1991. Who was he?

CAN'T ANYONE PLAY THIS GAME II, 1991–1996

1. He was the first baseman on the Mets in 1991 and is a cousin of Yankees star and Seattle manager Lou Pinella. Who is he?

2. He was the catcher for the Mets in 1991, but this New Jersey native spent his best years at Yankee Stadium. Who was he?

3. The Mets picked this speedster up from the Cardinals in 1991 and thought he would steal bases for them that year, he would end up being more of a liability to the team than an asset. Who was he?

4. He played shortstop for the Mets in 1991 and later played for the Yankees, Phillies, and Texas Rangers. Who was he?

5. This former catcher and manager of the Chicago White Sox became the Mets manager in 1992. Who was he?

6. The Mets picked up this Bronx native and former Pirate who took to wearing ear plugs during the 1992 season so he wouldn't hear the boo birds at Shea. Who was he?

7. In August of 1992 this pitcher, who had been a mainstay of the Mets, was traded to Toronto for infielder Jeff Kent and outfielder Ryan Thompson. Who was he?

8. This Mets hurler set a major league record of 27 consecutive defeats during the 1992 and 1993 season. Who was he?

    A: Frank Viola

    B: Sid Fernandez

    C: Frank Tanana

    D: Anthony Young

    E: Pete Schourek

9. This outfielder and Arkansas native rejoined the Mets from the Kansas City Royals during the 1994 season in exchange for Vince Coleman. Who was he?

10. What former Phillies hurler succeeded Jeff Torborg as the Mets manager during the 1993 season?

11. What Mets outfielder was suspended for tossing firecrackers at fans outside of Dodger stadium?

12. This veteran first baseman pounded 27 home runs and knocked in 100 runs for the hapless last place Mets during the 1993 season. Who was he?

13. This slugger would have his personal best in home runs with 34 for the Mets during the 1993 season. Who was he?

14. What son of a former major league pitcher played first base for the Mets during the 1994 season?

15. Who was the ace pitcher for the Mets with a 14–4 mark during the strike-shortened 1994 season?

16. What former Tiger went 5 for 5 for the Mets in a 1994 game against the Cardinals?

    A: Jose Vizcaino

    B: Rico Brogna

    C: Ryan Thompson

    D: Jay Burnitz

    E: Mel Watkins

17. Which 1994 Mets rookie tossed a shutout in his second start in the majors?

    A: Mike Remlinger

    B: Eric Hillman

    C: Joe Rinaldi

    D: Jason Jacome

    E: Jason Isringhausen

18. Who finished near the top in voting for NL Rookie of the Year, polishing off a 9–2 record with an ERA of 2.81 during his first year in the bigs?

19. What veteran centerfielder hit .311 and stole 21 bases for the Mets in the 1995 campaign?

20. Name the team the Mets picked up Lance Johnson from via free agency?

    A: the Indians

    B: the Cubs

    C: the White Sox

    D: the Cardinals

    E: the Tigers

21. Edgardo Alfonzo is a native of what country?

    A: Mexico

    B: Puerto Rico

    C: Venezuela

    D: Domican Republic

    E: Colombia

STIRRINGS, 1996–1998

1. In April 1996 during a game against this Eastern division foe, John Franco became the first southpaw to save 300 games. What team was it?

    A: Montreal

    B: Chicago

    C: Philadelphia

    D: Pittsburgh

2. Name the Mets player who went 5 for 5 and hit for the cycle against the Phillies in a 1996 game?

3. What Mets player stole home in a 1996 game against the Pirates?

   A: Bernard Gilkey

   B: Carlos Baerga

   C: Butch Huskey

   D: Lance Johnson

   E: Carl Everett

4. Whose record did Todd Hundley break when he set the record for most home runs hit by a catcher during the 1996 season?

5. What team was Rico Brogna traded to in November 1996?

   A: the Indians

   B: the Phillies

   C: the Astros

   D: the Padres

   E: the Pirates

6. Who were the two pitchers the Mets acquired in the Rico Brogna trade?

7. What NL team was Jerry Dipoto traded to in November 1996?

8. Why did Butch Huskey choose to wear jersey number 42 when he joined the Mets in 1995?

9. True or False: Bobby Valentine also played for the Mets in the '70s.

10. What Mets pitcher was the first NL hurler to reach 10 wins in the 1997 season?

11. What team did Bernard Gilkey leave to join the Mets in 1996?

12. What AL team did Lance Johnson play for before putting on Mets pinstripes?

13. The Mets attained Carlos Baerga from Cleveland in the 1996 season by trading two of their established players. Who were they?

14. Who was the Mets first opponent in interleague play 1997?

15. What was the outcome of that game?

16. Who won the first interleague series between the Mets and Red Sox in 1997?

17. What was the outcome of the first Mets–Yankees regular season game?

18. How did the Mets fare in the first interleague series with the Yankees?

19. Who was given three intentional walks in a 1997 game to tie an NL record?
    A: Todd Hundley
    B: Edgardo Alfonzo
    C: Keith Hernandez
    D: Mike Piazza
    E: Bobby Jones

20. Who replaced the injured Todd Hundley prior to the 1997 All-Star Game and hit a home run in his first game behind the plate for the 1997 Mets?

1998–2001

1. Who posted the highest season batting average in Mets history with .354 during the 1998 season?
    A: John Olerud
    B: Mike Piazza
    C: Butch Huskey
    D: Lance Johnson
    E: Todd Hundley

2. Where did the Mets finish in the 1998 season?
3. What Brooklyn High School did John Franco attended?
    A: Abraham Lincoln
    B: James Madison
    C: Canarsie
    D: Lafayette
    E: Sheepshead Bay
4. Who stole 66 bases for the Mets in the 1999 season?
5. What team did the Mets acquire Mike Piazza from in 1998?
6. Jay Payton was a teammate of Nomar Garciaparra at what college?
    A: USC
    B: Michigan State
    C: Georgia Tech
    D: Missouri
    E: Texas
7. What Mets hitter batted .400 in 20 at bats during the 2000 World Series?
    A: Edgardo Alfonzo
    B: Mike Piazza
    C: Todd Zeile
    D: Jay Payton
    E: Derek Bell
8. Who was the Mets only winning pitcher in the 2000 World Series?
    A: Al Leiter
    B: John Franco
    C: Rick Reed
    D: Bobby Jones
    E: Armando Benitez
9. Who did the Mets defeat in the 2000 NLCS?
10. What is Mike Piazza's jersey number?

EXTRA INNINGS

1. Who is the Mets all-time home run leader?
   A: Todd Hundley
   B: Keith Hernandez
   C: Gary Carter
   D: Darryl Strawberry
   E: Willie Mays
   F: Mike Piazza
2. Who has the most Met career wins for the Mets with 198?
   A: Jerry Koosman
   B: Dwight Gooden
   C: Tom Seaver
   D: Ron Darling
   E: Warren Spahn
3. Who holds the record for most career hits during his Mets career?
   A: Cleon Jones
   B: Ed Kranepool
   C: Mookie Wilson
   D: Keith Hernandez
   E: Lee Mazzilli
4. Name the four former Mets pitchers who pitched no-hitters *after* leaving the team.
5. Which Mets have won the MVP Award?
6. Name the Mets players who have won the NL Rookie of the Year Award.
7. How many times did Tom Seaver win the Cy Young Award?
8. Tom Seaver set the Mets seasonal strikeout record in 1971 with how many?
   A: 283
   B: 305

C: 289

D: 300

E: 291

9. Name the four men who managed both the Mets and Yankees.

10. Who was the first Met to get three hits in an All-Star game?

A: Lance Johnson

B: Jim Hickman

C: Lee Mazzilli

D: Cleon Jones

E: Keith Hernandez

11. Name the first two Mets players to have 100 plus RBI seasons in the same season?

12. What was the first season the Mets hosted an All-Star game?

13. He played in more games than any Mets player in their history. Who was he?

A: Tom Seaver

B: Bud Harrelson

C: Rusty Staub

D: Mookie Wilson

E: Ed Kranepool

14. True or false: The Mets went over the three-million mark in attendance at home during their history.

15. In their memorable maiden season of 1962 the Mets set their all-time losing streak of how many games?

A: 17

B: 15

C: 22

D: 12

E: 18

16. This Mets hurler pitched in 80 games during 1999, which

is a Mets record for most appearances in a season. Who was he?

    A: Doug Sisk

    B: John Franco

    C: Jeff Innis

    D: Turk Wendell

    E: Anthony Young

17. Who holds the Mets' record for most stolen bases in a season?

    A: Felix Millan

    B: Vince Coleman

    C: Len Dykstra

    D: Howard Johnson

    E: Mookie Wilson

18. Which manager holds the Mets' record for most wins with 595?

    A: Yogi Berra

    B: Bobby Valentine

    C: Casey Stengel

    D: Davey Johnson

    E: Gil Hodges

19. Who served the Mets for a record 11 years as their general manager?

Answers

ANSWERS: OH, THOSE EARLY YEARS!

1. The Mets took orange from the New York Giants and the blue from the Brooklyn Dodgers.
2. Casey Stengel
3. The Polo Grounds
4. Duke Snider
5. Richie Ashburn
6. Frank Thomas
7. Gil Hodges
8. Roger Craig
9. The Houston Colt .45s who later were renamed the Astros.
10. A painful 120 games.
11. Jimmy Piersall
12. Ron Hunt
13. Ed Kranepool
14. The Mets had two 20-games losers in 1962. Roger Craig led the league with 24 losses. Al Jackson lost 20, and Jay Hook was right behind with 19 losses.

15. Rogers Hornsby
16. Tracy Stallard
17. True. Yogi played in 4 games for the Mets in 1965 and got 2 hits in 9 at bats.
18. Wes Westrum
19. Casey Stengel played the outfield for the New York Giants in the '20s. He managed the Brooklyn Dodgers from 1934 through 1936. Stengel managed the Yankees from 1949–1960 and the Mets from 1962–1965.
20. Ralph Kiner, Lindsay Nelson, and Bob Murphy
21. Warren Spahn
22. Clarence Coleman
23. C: Hobie Landrith
24. B: The St. Louis Cardinals
25. C: Gus Bell
26. D: Gil Hodges
27. A: Al Jackson
28. The Giants
29. Marvin Eugene Throneberry
30. C: Willie Stargell
31. The Mets finished with a 66–95 record in 1966. The first season since their inception that they lost fewer than 100 games during a season.
32. 1967
33. Tommy Davis, who hit .302 in 1967.
34. A: Jim Bunning
35. D: 16 wins
36. Bud Harrelson
37. Gil Hodges managed the Washington Senators.
38. 1968
39. A: Nolan Ryan
40. Rheingold
41. Joan Payson
42. Number 37

ANSWERS: BUILDING SOMETHING AND THE MIRACLE AT FLUSHING MEADOWS

1. Jerry Koosman
2. Tommie Agee
3. Number 14
4. D: Astros
5. 1969
6. Also 1969
7. A: Dick Stuart
8. Phil Linz
9. D: Astros
10. Donn Clendenon
11. E: Cleon Jones hit .340 in 1969.
12. B: Cubs
13. Steve Carlton
14. C: 38
15. A: 25
16. B: Tom Seaver
17. D: Jimmy Qualls
18. B: Cleon Jones
19. D: 100
20. D: Tommie Agee
21. Ken Boswell
22. Wayne Garrett
23. C: Braves
24. True
25. A: Orioles
26. False. The Mets won it in five.
27. Jerry Koosman
28. Al Weis
29. Tommie Agee
30. Davey Johnson
31. C&G: Donn Clendenon and Al Weis shared the award.

32. A: 29
33. Gary Gentry
34. Tommie Agee

ANSWERS: BETWEEN PENNANTS, 1970–1972 AND YA GOTTA BELIEVE

1. C: The Mets finished in third place in 1970.
2. Ken Singleton
3. Amos Otis
4. B: 85
5. A: 19
6. B: the Expos
7. Jim Fregosi
8. Yogi Berra
9. Willie Mays
10. Rusty Staub
11. D: John Milner
12. D: Jon Matlack
13. A: the Braves
14. B: Tug McGraw
15. Number 24
16. Lawrence
17. Bob Aspromonte
18. Rusty Staub
19. Charlie Williams
20. Cincinnati, Los Angeles, and San Francisco.
21. False. The San Diego Padres had a lower batting average than the Mets .246: San Diego batsman hit at a .244 clip.
22. D .509
23. C: The St. Louis Cardinals finished a game and a half behind the Mets in the NL East in 1973.

24. A: John Milner
25. B: Felix Millan
26. E: the Reds
27. Pete Rose
28. D: Oakland
29. A: Willie Mays
30. C: Jon Matlack
31. A: Rusty Staub
32. Ron Hodges
33. George Theodore
34. George Stone
35. The Atlanta Braves

ANSWERS: YEARS OF STRUGGLE, 1974–1978

1. Nine
2. Joe Torre
3. A: Phillies
4. John Stearns
5. Dave Kingman
6. 22
7. Roy McMillan
8. Joe Frazier
9. Dave Kingman
10. C: Rusty Staub
11. E: Del Unser
12. Bob Apodoca
13. Mike Vail
14. Jesus
15. Jerry Koosman
16. Mickey Lolich
17. Pitcher Pat Zachry, infielder Doug Flynn, and outfielders Steve Henderson and Dan Norman.

18. Donald Grant
19. Dave Kingman
20. Joe Torre
21. Len Randle
22. Steve Henderson, John Milner, and John Stearns.
23. Torre played for the Braves and the Cardinals.
24. Abraham Lincoln
25. D: Minnesota
26. Willie Montantez
27. Nino Espinosa

ANSWERS: THE AGONY CONTINUES, 1978–1983

1. The Philadelphia Phillies
2. Elliot Maddox
3. Joel Youngblood
4. D: Craig Swan
5. The Baltimore Orioles
6. Richie Hebner
7. Fred Wilpon
8. Claudell Washington
9. A: Mark Bomback
10. Jeff Reardon
11. Most consecutive games hit safely in by a National League player, it was by Pete Rose with thirty-eight.
12. George Bamberger
13. George Foster
14. Dave Kingman
15. B: Hubie Brooks
16. Mookie Wilson
17. Ron Darling and Walt Terrell
18. A: Tom Seaver

19. Mike Torrez
20. D: Darryl Strawberry
21. Neil Allen and Rick Owenby
22. Frank Howard
23. Rusty Staub
24. D: George Foster
25. Hernandez won it in 1979 with a .344 batting average.

ANSWERS: BUILDING SOMETHING, 1984–1985

1. Davey Johnson
2. E: The Chicago White Sox
3. A: The Los Angeles Dodgers
4. Number 18
5. Number 17
6. Mex
7. Ed Lynch
8. Number 17
9. B: Keith Hernandez
10. Dwight Gooden
11. The Mets finished in second place, six games behind the Cubs.
12. Bruce Berenyi
13. Calvin Schiraldi
14. In honor of his native state of Hawaii—the 50th state to be admitted to the Union.
15. D: Jerry Orosco
16. Number 8
17. Rusty Staub
18. The Montreal Expos
19. The Atlanta Braves
20. The St. Lous Cardinals

21. D: 24
22. Number 16
23. 32
24. A: Gary Carter

ANSWERS: THAT WONDERFUL YEAR, 1986

1. The Mets won 108 games in the regular season in 1986.
2. Bobby Ojeda
3. Darryl Strawberry
4. Ray Knight
5. Lenny Dykstra
6. Lee Mazzilli
7. Kevin Mitchell
8. Chicago Cubs
9. 21½ games
10. The Phillies
11. Bob Ojeda, with 18 wins.
12. Rafael Santana
13. William Hayward Wilson
14. Roger McDowell and Jesse Orosco
15. Wally Backman
16. The Houston Astros
17. Mike Scott
18. A: Lenny Dykstra
19. D: 16

ANSWERS: THE 1986 WORLD SERIES

1. Ron Darling
2. Boston Red Sox
3. John McNamara

4. Tom Seaver
5. Tim Teufel let a ground ball go through his legs that allowed the Red Sox to score the one run of the game.
6. B: Bruce Hurst
7. Ron Darling
8. C: Kevin Mitchell
9. E: Bob Stanley
10. Bill Buckner
11. D: Ray Knight
12. A: Ron Darling
13. B: Bruce Hurst
14. B: Ray Knight
15. Jerry Orosco
16. Marty Barrett, who had 13 hits for the Boston during the series.
17. Ed Koch
18. Ray Knight

ANSWERS: CLOSE BUT NO CIGAR, 1987–1990

1. Kevin McReynolds
2. Ray Knight
3. The Mets finished second, three games behind the Cardinals.
4. Dwight Gooden
5. Darryl Strawberry
6. David Cone
7. Howard Johnson
8. C: David Cone
9. False. The Mets had 100 wins in the 1988 season.
10. Gregg Jefferies
11. The Los Angeles Dodgers

12. The Mets lost in seven games.
13. Juan Samuel
14. Frank Viola
15. Howard Johnson
16. The Chicago Cubs
17. Randy Myers
18. E: Frank Viola
19. A: Pittsburgh
20. Bud Harrelson
21. John Franco
22. Darryl Strawberry

ANSWERS: CAN'T ANYONE PLAY THIS GAME II, 1991–1996

1. Dave Magadan
2. Rick Cerone
3. Vince Coleman
4. Kevin Elster
5. Jeff Torborg
6. Bobby Bonilla
7. David Cone
8. D: Anthony Young
9. Kevin McReynolds
10. Dallas Green
11. Vince Coleman
12. Eddie Murray
13. Bobby Bonilla
14. David Sequi
15. Bret Saberhagen
16. B: Rico Brogna
17. D: Jason Jacome

18. Jason Isringhausen
19. Brett Butler
20. C: The Chicago White Sox
21. C: Venezuela

ANSWERS: STIRRINGS, 1996–1998

1. A: Montreal
2. Alex Ochea
3. C: Butch Huskey
4. Roy Campanella
5. B: Phillies
6. Toby Borland and Ricardo Jordan
7. The Colorado Rockies
8. In honor of Jackie Robinson.
9. True. Valentine played for the Mets in the 1977–1978 seasons.
10. Bobby Jones
11. The St. Louis Cardinals
12. The Chicago White Sox
13. Jeff Kent and Jose Vizcaino
14. The Mets and the Boston Red Sox played on the night of June 13, 1997.
15. The Red Sox beat the Mets 8–4.
16. The Red Sox, two games to one.
17. The Mets defeated the Yankees 6–0 at Yankee Stadium on June 16, 1997.
18. The Yankees took the series two games to one.
19. A: Todd Hundley
20. Todd Pratt
21. A: .279

ANSWERS: 1998–2001

1. John Olerud
2. Second in the NL East.
3. D: Lafayette High School in Brooklyn.
4. Roger Cedeño
5. The Florida Marlins
6. C: Georgia Tech
7. C: Todd Zeile
8. John Franco
9. The St. Louis Cardinals
10. Number 31

ANSWERS: EXTRA INNINGS

1. D: Darryl Strawberry with 252 dingers.
2. C: Tom Seaver
3. B: Ed Kranepool
4. Tom Seaver with the Reds, Nolan Ryan with the Angels, Astros, and Rangers. Dwight Gooden and David Cone with the Yankees.
5. As of 2001 no Met has ever won the award.
6. Tom Seaver in 1967, Jon Matlack in 1972, Darryl Strawberry in 1983, and Dwight Gooden in 1984.
7. Three times, 1969, 1973, and 1975.
8. C: 289
9. Casey Stengel, Yogi Berra, Joe Torre, and Dallas Green.
10. A: Lance Johnson
11. Todd Hundley and Bernard Gilkey, in 1996.
12. 1964
13. E: Ed Kranepool, 1,853 games.
14. True. 1987–1988

15. 17 consecutive games from May 21–June 6, 1962.
16. Turk Wendell
17. Mookie Wilson, with 281 stolen bases.
18. D: Davey Johnson
19. Frank Cashen, from 1980–1991.